Isaac Adams

Darkness and Daybreak

Personal Experiences, Manners, Customs, Habits, Religious and Social Life in Persia

Isaac Adams

Darkness and Daybreak
Personal Experiences, Manners, Customs, Habits, Religious and Social Life in Persia

ISBN/EAN: 9783337292478

Printed in Europe, USA, Canada, Australia, Japan

Cover: Foto ©Andreas Hilbeck / pixelio.de

More available books at **www.hansebooks.com**

Darkness and Daybreak.

(Romans xiii: 12.)

Personal Experiences, Manners, Customs, Habits,
Religious and Social Life in
Persia.

by

REV. ISAAC ADAMS.

—

Published in the interest of Persian
Mission.

1898.

PREFACE.

THE author of this little volume, "DARKNESS AND DAYBREAK," is a native of Persia, who is known to us more than four years. Mr. Adams has been with us in intimate association, in religious exercises and social life, and all who know him can bear testimony to the purity and unselfishness of his character, to his earnestness and laboriousness as a student, to his intense zeal for the spread of the gospel of our Lord Jesus Christ in Persia and the world, and to the wrongs and sufferings and lost condition of his people.

This work serves a useful purpose in imparting fresh information and quickening an intelligent interest of a hopeful Christian effort. We hope that no student of the Kingdom, no servant of Christ and his Church should fail to give serious and sympathetic attention to the spread of the gospel in helping our dear brother Isaac Adams, and we trust every reader will join us in the hope and prayer and sympathy and substantial help that the way may soon be open for his return as a missionary of the cross and enter the work which he has already begun.

PROF. G. K. HEMKES,
Rector of the Christian Reformed Theological School.

GRAND RAPIDS, MICH., U. S. A.
April 4th, 1898.

DEAR READER:

I cannot begin to write a narrative of the facts connected with the history of my life, without giving all glory and praise to the most precious God, who has so wonderfully guided me, during the last ten years especially. No words like those of the Scriptures can adequately express my heart's gratitude for all the ways by which he has led me, and you, dear reader, will magnify him while reading as I did while writing this. Let us exalt His name forever; let the Lord be magnified, which taketh pleasure in the prosperity of His elect. Praise ye the Lord, for His name is excellent; His glory is above the heavens. I have been deeply tried; yes, the Lord is with the righteous; "Lo, I am with you." Surely He has been with me; His presence has gone before me and has given me strength and courage. He faileth not. I have heard his voice saying, "Fear not, I will help thee." And He has done so; yea, in the deepest waters; in all places His hand has led me and He has kept me. With David I can say, "God is my salvation." I will trust and not be afraid. I cried by reason of my affliction unto the Lord, and he answered me. The Lord stood by me and strengthened me, saying: "My strength is made perfect in weakness."

From many dangerous snares hath the Lord preserved me; in spite of all my inward rebellion, He hath carried on his good work in my heart, and notwithstanding all my unbelieving fears he hath given me a hope full of immortality. He hath set my feet upon a rock and established my goings and hath put a new song into my mouth; even praises unto my God.

The same grace and forbearance, the same wisdom and power that have brought me so far, will bring me on, though it be through fire and water, to a goodly heritage. I see no business in life but the work of Christ, neither do I desire any employment to all eternity but His service, and it is my prayer to Him, in whose hands the hearts of all men are like the rivers of water, that He might put into the hearts of those who love Him and His cause to enable me to continue in His service by bringing the knowledge of the only Redeemer Jesus Christ to the great multitude who know Him not.

PERSONAL HISTORY.

I WAS born in the northwestern part of Persia, on the twenty-eighth day of November, 1872, at Sangar, a village about two hours walk from Oroomiah city. The village contained about twenty-five Nestorian families, and as many houses. The surrounding villages were all Mohammedan, some of them lying not more than half an hour's distance away from Sangar. Thus the people in my village-home have had all their intercourse with Mohammedans, and in consequence had lost all knowledge of Christianity and had adopted instead Mohammedan customs as well as their language, the national language of the Nestorians being Syriac, which is widely different from that of the Mohammadans. Together with the customs and language, the people of my home-village had also adopted all kinds of profanity. The keeping of the Sabbath day was entirely lost. People would plow and do other work in the field just as on any other day.

Another very bad habit of the people at Sangar was the beating of their wives. It is quite common there to see a woman's head bruised and her clothing torn. Thus I was brought up, among ignorant and ill-influenced people.

When about 6 years of age, my father and two other persons went to Russia for the trading business. They had but one passport for the three of them. After having remained in Russia for a short time, one of the men was obliged to return to Persia, he having been advised of sickness in his family. After some time, my father and his companion were to go on to another city in Russia. Upon entering the gates they were taken prisoners, the officer claiming that in the passport three men were mentioned, and they were but two. All explanation on the part of the travelers was unheeded, and their case was finally ended by sending them both to Siberia for life, and in all probability they are already dead, as we have never heard of them since.

It was extremely sad for my poor mother to have been left with five children, all below 12 years of age; but this was not all. The lord of the village came with some forged notes, claiming that my father owed him money and demanding pay. As my mother had nothing to pay with, he took possession of the land we owned and a part of our vineyard.

My task in early boyhood was to do little chores at home and herd cattle. Like most boys, I delighted in climbing trees, but once it happened that I fell from the top of a tree and broke my arm. Blood was gushing from my nose and ears, and I was carried home. The house was soon crowded with people, who decided to make bread and Martooha and give it as a sacrifice to the poor.

The Martooha is a mixture of flour, molasses and butter, and is received by those among whom it is distributed as an offering, with the greeting: "May God restore him to health."

But this was not all. My mother had also secretly, but solemnly, vowed that she would, in case of my recovery, have a lamb sacrificed to Mar-Obdishoo, a Nestorian saint, at the church built to his memory. When I was quite recovered, therefore, my mother, a number of friends and I, with a lamb, repaired to Mar-Obdishoo. The lamb was slain in the church-yard and its blood sprinkled on the altar of the church and in my face, while a number of little bells were rung in the church. I was then ordered to take the bells, and, ringing them, cry out: "O, Mar-Obdishoo, Mar-Obdishoo, I thank you that you have let me regain my health!"

The lamb was hereupon taken to a dwelling and boiled, and the meat given to those in attendance; the head and skin, however, together with a small quantity of meat, belonged to the janitor as his fee. Some of the meat was also taken back to Sangar, upon our return, to be distributed there. I was not allowed one morsel of it.

When about 13 years of age, a buffalo out of the herd of cattle I was watching, ran among some heaps of cut wheat in a field where farmers were threshing. In doing so, the buffalo broke the Dach, or sign, which the lord of the village had set upon the heaps of wheat. Upon perceiving this, the lord called me to him in a very friendly manner, holding out to me a very beautiful cane and promising me the cane if I came. I did so, though hesitatingly. Suddenly I was rudely seized by some servants who held me firmly, while others subjected me to an application of the bastinado, so cruelly, that both my feet bled profusely and I was not able to walk for about two months.

After this sad experience I left the village clandestinely and repaired to Wazerawa, where my aunt and all the relatives of my mother lived. My aunt received me gladly, and, having lost a child of about my age, bade me remain with her and would not hear of my leaving. After I had been with her for about one year the rest of our family followed to Wazerawa.

At Sangar we had owned an orchard near the dwelling where we lived. It had been my delight to climb into the fruit trees and eat fruit to my heart's content. Near my aunt's dwelling, at Wazerawa, there also was an orchard, but it belonged to a neighbor. This difference in ownership, however, made very little difference to me, and I tried to continue my orchard practice here also. Of course, I well knew that I deserved punishment for climbing into a neighbor's tree and appropriating some of the fruit, consequently I did my tree-climbing after dark, in the evening. One dark night, as I sat in the very top of a fine apple tree, feeling quite secure from detection, I suddenly heard a voice below me calling out: "What are you doing up there?" I replied that I had been late for supper, for which my uncle would whip me. I had, therefore, tried to hide from him. He ordered me to come down, but my pockets were filled with apples from the tree, and so I hesitated, pondering how to escape the well-deserved punishment.

Finally I told the neighbor I would come down if he would promise not to chastise me. He did so; and I came down, delivered up my stolen apples and went home.

My uncle now began to employ me by sending me out to his vineyard to watch it. I had very good times doing this, as I was very liberal. I would stand out in the road and ask people passing by to come in and help themselves to some grapes, and quite often I pressed my request so urgently as to almost compel people to come in and eat grapes. Occasionally I would fill a basket with grapes and hand out some to every person who happened to pass by. My motive in doing this was that I considered it an injustice that I alone should have so many fine grapes, while so many others had none. The principal reason for my liberality, however, was my sociability. I liked to be in company with other human beings and hated seclusion. The neighbors surrounding my uncle's vineyard were all Mohammedans with whom I dared not communicate, and I, therefore, sought, by being liberal, to enjoy the company of, and intercourse with, fellow-beings such as I myself was.

The vineyard was a very quiet, secluded spot, and I could not even force myself into liking it. When my mother and the rest of the family moved to Wazerawa, I consequently left my uncle's and joined a number of other young lads in taking care of herds of cattle and flocks of sheep.

While being thus occupied one day, a boy, Benyamin Bar Younan by name, a relative to Kasha Sayad, a native preacher, employed by the Presbyterian mission in Persia, met me. He remained with me for some time, repeating to me stories from the Bible, among others the parable of the rich man and Lazarus. When he had left me I could not help but think over and over again what I had heard. A few days later we met a second time. I addressed him with this question: "Suppose a man should like to go to heaven, what must he do?" He replied: "He must not eat or drink anything for three days, but keep on in prayer all this time, and then be good and do good afterwards. "Then," said I, "the people must be very foolish not to prefer to be like Lazarus in this life, when heaven and its blessedness last forever." I then asked where he had found those stories, and what other knowledge he had of heaven. He told me it was all written in a book called Bible, which he claimed to be a very holy book, even called it God's book; but also told me that, if I wished to learn more about these things, I should have to go and see his uncle, Kasha Sayad. I followed this advice, for I was eager to learn more, and to Kasha Sayad I am greatly indebted for what knowledge I received by my early acquaintance with him. Through his influence I was enabled to attend the missionary school, where my hungry and thirsty soul was fed on the precious word of God. Reading my Testament, and not being able to comprehend very much of it at first, I would kneel down and pray to God, and say: "O Lord, if

13

Thou art God, make Thyself manifest and show me also myself." Then again at times it seemed almost impossible to me to trust fully in an invisible God.

Upon entering the mission school I encountered the enmity and hatred of my relatives, who were all dissatisfied with this step; but, by the grace of God and through the kindness of Kasha Sayad, I was enabled to attend also the high school at Oroomiah City, a Presbyterian institute.

Here I attended until the winter of 1887, when I was requested by Kasha Peria, a native missionary, who had been educated at Hermansburg, Germany, and received his support from there, to go and teach one of his schools at Satlovi. I took charge of a school of about twenty-five children, and found the work very interesting, especially as I visited the children's parents in the evenings, and, to their great delight, read to them from the Bible. I did not try to give any explanations, but simply read from ten to fifteen consecutive chapters. On Saturdays I went to the neighboring villages with my Bible, read from it to the people and conversed with them on the Christian religion and Christ's love to sinners. Returning from such work towards evening one Saturday, I met a Mohammedan and passed without saluting him. He stopped me, and roughly inquired why I had not greeted him. I told him I had neglected the courtesy because I did not know in what language to address him. To explain this, I must inform the reader that not all Mohammedans speak the same language. It is also dangerous to address Mohammedans, as I had found by the following experience which I had had some time previous: I had met two Mohammedans on my way and saluted them both in a friendly manner. Presently there came a Christian. I stopped immediately and spoke to him. Upon perceiving this the two Mohammedans quickly returned, stopped me, and, one placing himself on my right side, the other on the left, each dagger in hand, they said they would immediately kill me if I did not at once return their salutation. I complied with their request so eagerly that I bowed three times to their once. In this instance the Mohammedan was not satisfied, but insisted that I had failed to greet him through disrespect and threatened also to kill me, accompanying this threat by a drawn dagger, the point of which he pressed to my breast so hard that I even felt the point penetrating my skin. But at that moment we saw a caravan approaching, whereupon the Mohammedan withdrew his dagger and contemptuously said that he had only tried to scare me.

.I was so excited that I could not speak for four or five hours, was taken to a village near by and remained there until Monday; then I returned and continued my work.*

In the summer of 1887 I entered Oroomiah College Mission School, in connection with which there is also an industrial school. At the latter, carpenter's work, shoemaking and hatmaking were taught. I, in connection with my other studies, entered the shoemaking department, and under the direction of Oosta Ayraham learned that trade. After a few weeks, during which Mr. Ayraham had become acquainted with me and my circumstances, he took more pains with me than with any other of his pupils, so that in the examination at the end of the term I made a good showing.

The college term ended in July; this permitted me to devote all my time to my trade in the industrial school. In the fall of 1888, Mr. Ayraham left his position. A Mohammedan took his place. During the

---

*This Mohammedan's name was Samat of Baranduz. Before my encounter with him he had already killed not less than sixty persons. He was about 40 years of age and was later on killed by other robbers.

vacancy the school was left in my charge. I had possession of the keys, and the whole property was in my care. The new teacher gave no satisfaction; he appeared to be dishonest, and was soon discharged. I then again filled the position until another teacher could be found.

After the closing of the college term, I kept the industrial school in operation. I was in charge of from ten to fifteen boys, and the work progressed nicely in the interest of the mission. During this time I was also elected elder in the church at Wazerawa, and while at college I spent every Sunday at Wazerawa and Dizza, teaching Sunday school. I was also robbed several times and had several dangerous encounters with highwaymen, one of which has left me a scar on my right eye to this day.

In the spring of 1889, I was sent by the missionaries to teach a school at Ardishai. I had here forty pupils on an average, coming from about six different villages. The instruction was to be given in four different languages, viz: Persian, Turkish, Chaldean and Syriac. But I must confess I was rather severe in my treatment with the pupils. I generally kept about a half dozen switches in the school-room, and it was not at all uncommon for me to whip children until they bled. I kept all doors and windows closed, to stifle the screams of the poor children while being chastised, but the boys nevertheless managed to make themselves be heard for about two blocks. I thought then that I had to do this, since the parents in place of administering the proper punishment at home, would come and tell me that their children had sinned and entreated me to punish them for it.

One day as I rang the bell, it appeared to me the pupils had made up their minds to have their own way about coming. The rule was that, upon hearing the bell ring, every pupil should drop everything and come

ISAAC ADAMS,
In High-class Costume.

DAVID ADAMS,
In Mohammedan Priest
Costume.

ABRAHAM ADAMS,
In Kurdish Costume.

JACOB ADAMS,
In Common Persian Costume.

PAUL JOHN.   Page 33.

right into the school-room and quietly take his seat. I said nothing, but waited. When they came in, about five minutes later, I shut all doors and windows and ordered them to stand side by side with their backs against the wall. I then took a switch, rushed around the room and struck them again and again across their bare legs and feet (their shoes and slippers always were left standing out in the hall). Soon legs and feet began to bleed, and of course they screamed piteously. But this I would not have. To stop it I struck some of them, who had fallen to the floor, across their backs, and threatened to treat them all in the same manner if they did not immediately cease their noise. By this outrage I soon had the room quieted, and the pupils were always on time afterwards. This, however, was not the only mode of punishment. Sometimes I would order the tallest boy in the room to take the boy who was to be chastised, on his back, holding him by his hands, and then bend over to keep his feet from the ground. I would then take my switch and lash the boy across his legs and back. Still another severe chastisement is to have the pupil fold his arms tightly and then sit down upon the floor. A stick is now passed through under his arms in front of his body, his legs then are lifted over the stick and he is thus left in a helpless position, so that the teacher may strike him wherever he pleases. Occasionally I was afraid inwardly of some of the boys, as they were older and taller than I was, but somehow I overcame the sensation, and never had any trouble in this direction. I was not the originator or inventor of any of these cruel modes of punishment. I had myself learned them by seeing them practiced, and many times at the high-school I myself had been ordered to hold a boy across my back, being somewhat taller and stronger than some of the rest.

But now I have a different way of administering punishment in my schools; not with a switch, but with love and kindness, and I think I can accomplish more with kind words and acts than with the rod. This is one of the changes I have experienced since having come to America.

Besides teaching languages, I also gave instruction from the Bible, in arithmetic and geography. I also visited the parents of the pupils, together with the minister of the village, and on Sabbath day I had a large class of ladies in the Sunday school.

I would also pay visits to other villages and preach to them in a very simple manner, only repeating to the people the story of the cross. While engaged in this manner one day, I read in my Bible the 12th chapter of Genesis. This gave me much thought, especially the passage where the Lord said to Abraham, " Get thee out of thy country and from thy kindred and from thy father's house into a land that I will show thee." My strain of thought on this matter ran in this channel: "If Abraham obeyed this command of the Lord, and I am now worshipping the same Lord as Abraham then was, why should I not follow his example, now reading the same command?"

I consulted Kasha Sayad, and informed him of my intention to go somewhere where I could prepare for Christian work. His opinion was, that it would not be a wise step for me to take, and bade me go to a missionary and lay the matter before him. I did so, and the missionary gave me many reasons why I should abandon such thoughts; but I was determined to rather listen to God's promises than man's advices and go, whither he should direct me.

In July, 1889, I left Oroomiah with not more than what amounts to five dollars in the United States, and not knowing where I should finally land. I traveled westward, but it was a long and tedious journey. As I had no means to hire a horse or mule I was obliged to walk, and for the sake of convenience I often traveled during the night, it being then much cooler.

After nineteen days of traveling, I reached the first railway in the Caucasus in Russia. I reached the first railway station at Akistafa. From here I was given free transportation to Tiflis. There some Christians helped me on to Valadikokas. After having arrived at this place I tried to work and go to school, but after a few weeks they urged me to go to Berlin, as they thought I might there succeed better in both. After seven or eight days travel I reached the boundary line of Russia. Here I bought a ticket to Berlin, while my passport was in the office for examination. Soon I was informed that I could not leave Russia, as my passport was defective. I was imprisoned for three days without food or drink, after which time I was ordered to telegraph to St. Petersburg for a permit to leave the country. I did so, and was obliged to pay an exorbitant sum for the dispatch. But no answer came from St. Petersburg. I was now informed that I would be sent to Siberia. It seemed a little hard to me at first, but thinking of the errand upon which I had set out on my journey, I concluded that the Lord wanted me there, if he would allow me to be sent there. I consequently told the officers that I was ready and willing to go. The officers obviously knew not what to make of this, for they stared at me as though they considered me a lunatic. They wished to know why I was so ready and willing to go to such a dismal country as Siberia. I told them that if my Lord and God desired me to go there, I certainly was most willing to go, as I sincerely believed that he was in Siberia as well as in Berlin; that years ago my father had been sent there without cause, and I might perchance meet him there. When they saw I cared so little whither I went, they even helped me on to Berlin.

Here I was in Berlin, the great German capital, not being able to speak or even understand a word of the language. But through God's kind providence I encountered a young man who was able to speak five or six different languages, namely, Turkish, Syriac, German, etc. He grew very friendly to me, took me to his room, provided me with a good place to live, and for several days showed me the sights in the city. He incidentally spoke of me to a friend who became so interested as to express a desire to see me. We consequently took supper at the house of this friend, Mr. L. H. O. Schmidt, west 62 Maasrein Strasse No. 31 Pa. Berlin, one evening, and by means of an interpreter I made this gentleman acquainted with my whole history. Mr. Schmidt, perhaps noticing a sad expression which had perchance overspread my countenance, bade me be of good cheer, for the Lord would certainly guide me and provide for me. To encourage me still more, he asked me to sit between himself and Mrs. Schmidt, as that, he thought, would make me feel more at home with them.

When we arose to take our departure from this hospitable house, Mr. Schmidt requested us to linger a few moments longer, and left the room. A few moments later he re-entered, and handed over to me a sum of money sufficient to go from Berlin to New York, at the same time remarking that he were quite certain, even if I remained in Berlin at present, I would certainly desire to see America in a few years hence, and so in his opinion it would be much better for me and my cause to go there at once. He also handed me a letter to a minister at Hamburg, by which I was introduced, and he requested to receive me and attend for me to all necessary requisites for a passage to New York City.

I left Berlin and reached Hamburg at about 11 o'clock
p. m. Not being able to explain to anyone where I wished
to go, I set out on a search for the dwelling of the minister to whom my letter of introduction was addressed.
I found the place at last, but the valet insisted upon
seeing my letter before he would allow me to go into
his house, fearing probably that I might be some thief
or robber trying to get admission. I, however, refused
to have my letter examined, as I mistrusted its being
returned to me. There was nothing left for me to do
but to go back to the depot. Here I found every door
locked and all the lights extinguished, and set out to
walk the streets until morning. But even in this I was
disturbed by patrolmen, who would not allow it. At last
I found a place where there was a cavity under the side-
walk, next to a basement window. I crept into this hole,
and doubling up as well as I could soon fell asleep.
When I awoke I was so stiff and numb, from the chilly
air and my inconvenient position, I could scarcely move.
I got up and out and ran along the streets to get warm.
After finding that the blood in my body was once more
circulating freely, I returned to my hiding place and
slept until daylight. I now returned to the minister's
dwelling, and he himself answering my rap at the door,
I handed him my letter. He was greatly surprised at
seeing me and learning who I was, and said that he had
been aware of my coming, but had not expected that I
would arrive on that train. He kindly ushered me into
the house, however, and after having washed, arranged
my toilet and breakfasted, he went with me to the
steamer that was to take me to New York City. After
procuring tickets we learned that the steamer would
not leave until two days later. I remained with the
reverend gentleman these two days, he proving very
kind and generous to me. Our conversations, however,
were very limited, as it had to be carried on entirely by

making use of the natural language—motions, signs, groans, expressions of the face, etc.

After two days, I boarded an ocean steamer for New York City. On the first and second day of the voyage the weather was fine and the sea tranquil and calm; but soon it became rough and I had an experience such as I had never heard of before—I grew sea-sick. During my misery I sometimes really took it for granted that all good Christian people had done for me ever since I had left home had been done merely for the purpose of severely punishing me for having been too bold and forward, and I asked the Lord in prayer to grant that the ship might capsize and sink, and so all my suffering be ended.

During our ocean voyage all passengers on board of the steamer were vaccinated. When my turn came I had hidden away, thinking my arm was to be cut off. I was compelled, however, to come forward and allow the operation to be performed on me, whereupon I found that it was not so bad after all.

Eighteen days after having gone aboard the steamer we arrived in New York City. In Castle Garden we were asked to show our money, there being a law that every person must have at least twenty-five dollars, to live on until able to find work, should he wish to enter the country; the company was obliged to take back any passenger who did not possess that amount. When my turn came to go through the gate, just when prepared to show the money I had (amounting to about twenty-eight cents), the officer was handed a letter by a boy. He stepped just a little to one side to quickly peruse the letter, but in the mean time I opened the gate and passed through unnoticed, and was soon lost in the crowd to any searching eye. I walked into the park and sat down. While looking around I suddenly espied a black man not far off. This was a great curiosity to me

22 -

who had never before seen colored people. I felt very much inclined to step nearer so as to get a better view of the man, but I dared not. Upon noticing many people passing by him without scarcely taking any notice of him, I also took heart and approached the black man. Seeing that his face, neck and arms were all black, I cocluded that this could not possibly be a human being. Since then I have met many negroes, have even lived among them for a year in Virginia, and have learned to esteem some of them as thoroughly, consecrated Christians.

Here I was once more all alone in a foreign country, without home, friends, acquaintances, or even means wherewith to support myself, almost utterly helpless, as I could not even make myself understood. For three days and nights I walked the streets of the great metropolis with an empty stomach. Towards the close of the third day I found a morsel of bread in an ash barrel. I took it out, cleaned it as well as I could, and then soaked it in some water and ate it. Not long after I also met a man who could understand oriental languages. This man proved a great blessing to me, for he had soon learned my situation. Feeling compassion for me, he fed me and then took me to the "Home of Children's Aid Society," No. 247 East Forty-fourth Street, corner Second Avenue.

The superintendent at the home, after hearing the circumstances, was gladly willing to admit me for a few days and try to procure me some work, it being against the rules of the institution to permanently admit persons of my age. In connection with this home there is also a brush shop where crippled boys are employed.

I was directed there and soon set to work. The superintendent was pleased and wish to retain me, so I worked during the day and attended a night school in the evening, where I studied the English language.

Sometimes, when visitors came, they would be very much surprised to see me, a sturdy, well-grown young fellow, working among crippled boys. This greatly irritated me, and, to avoid it, I walked lame whenever visitors came in after that.

But I could not remain in this place always. So I told the superintendent that I would rather work in the open air and not be confined so much within a building. Thereupon he sent me to a farm in New Jersey. I was there about two weeks when I was taken ill and had to give this up, the work being too hard for me as it consisted chiefly of chopping wood, it being in the midst of winter. In consequence of this experience I returned to my former occupation in the brush factory.

One day a lady called upon the superintendent and asked him if he could not recommend some one to her as a waiter. I happened to be in the room just then and the superintendent pointed me out to her. The lady inquired whether I would be willing to accept the position. I cheerfully answered in the affirmative and immediately accompanied her to her home. I could now make myself understood in English, somewhat, and the lady promised to give me further instruction. She was a sister to a physician, Dr. J. H. Cooley, and resided at Plainfield, N. J. I was in her service for three months and was pleased with my work, which consisted in waiting at the table and helping in the kitchen. Dr. Cooley also had a sanitarium, where patients were housed and taken care of. I am much indebted to the doctor for kindness in treating me as pleasantly as he did. During my stay at Plainfield, N. J., I wrote to Rev. J. H. Shadd, the missionary, whose acquaintance I had made in Persia, and who, I had been informed, was now in the United States on a visit. I asked him in my letter to kindly recommend me to some Presbyterian Church, which I might join. In answer to my request

Rev. Dr. Ketcham, rector at the First Presbyterian Church at Plainfield, received the following, to-wit:

MARIETTA, O., April 3, 1890.

REV. DR. KETCHAM.

DEAR BROTHER: Yours of April 1 has just come. Yesterday I sent a letter to the young man, which will give you the needed recommendation, and trust he may find a home in your church. There is a strong influence in New York to draw the young Nestorians to the Episcopalians and to the side of the Ritualist, who are at work in our mission field.

This young man has declined the strong temptation to leave the church in which he was raised, and I am glad he has sought you and your church, and trust you may do him good.

Yours very truly,

J. H. SHADD.

Dr. Ketcham and his congregation received me very cordially.

After three months stay at Plainfield, I deemed it advisable to go to New York City, there to improve my education; it being, however, two months previous to the beginning of a new term in any of the schools, I took recourse to Mr. Matthews, at that time superintendent of the "Children's Aid Society," for a place on a farm. A few days later another boy and I were sent to a farm in Orange county, New Jersey, with letters of recommendation for our introduction. We unhappily left the train at a station twelve miles this side of our place of destination. We did the best we could under the circumstances, however, stopped at the depot over night and started out afoot next morning. Finally, we arrived at the place where my companion had to leave me, as he was to work on some other farm. We parted and I trotted on alone. Presently I met a man coming towards me who inquired whither I was going. I showed him the address on my letter. He inquired further, what I intended to do there. After having told him, he informed me that this farmer had moved away, but that he had been looking for some help, and I might come and work for him. I inquired about the hire, and he offered fifteen dollars per month. I asked whether or not any churches were in his neighborhood. He said there were plenty of those things round about, whereupon I inquired into his religious views. He informed me of being a Roman Catholic by birth and education, "but," said he, sneeringly, "I have not been inside of a church for forty years." I hereupon offered to work for him for twelve dollars a month, provided he would not compel me to work on Sundays. He was satisfied, and I entered upon my duties. Later on I learned that the man I had been sent to, lived on the neighboring farm, and was a very nice man; not a very ugly fellow, as my present master had claimed at our first meeting.

My occupation on this farm consisted in cutting grass and milking cows, of which the farmer owned forty-five heads. Eighteen of them I had to milk, which at first caused such a strain upon the knuckles of my hands and on my wrists that I would wake up at night from pain in those parts; but I soon became accustomed to it, and then so much more enjoyed drinking my fill of the fresh milk, of which I was very fond. When once I had mentioned in a letter to my relatives at home that my work, among other things, consisted in milking cows, they wonderingly inquired in their next letter where in America the women might be and what they did, as in Persia all this kind of work is left to the women to perform.

For the first two weeks all went well with me on this farm. On Sunday I attended a Methodist Church. On the third Sunday, however, the farmer called me and ordered me to turn the crank on the grindstone for him, as he wished to sharpen his knife. I answered, "No, today is Sunday." Upon hearing this he cursed me and said: "I would rather sit here and listen to the dog barking than hear that minister preach."

At 4 o'clock in the morning he would call me to get up and go to work, but after some time he said, "Ike, you must get up at 3 o'clock, as the neighbors are out at that time;" and to make good his demand he would stamp on the steps of the stairway and pound the door, calling "Ike, Ike!" with an occasional curse intermingled, until he heard me move about.

One day we were loading hay in the field. My master was on the wagon, I stood upon the ground and pitched the hay to him. He kept swearing and cursing at me, trying to hurry me up. This provoked me, and I began to throw hay upon the wagon as fast as I could, without looking where I threw it. In so doing it happened that a pitchfork full of the hay, together with the points of the fork, struck him on the chest. At this he grew furious, jumped down from the wagon to the ground and tried to strike me, but I kept out of his reach.

While engaged in scattering hay upon a time, I came upon a heap in which there was a bee's nest. I noticed it in time, cautiously went by and left it untouched. The farmer, however, coming after me, but not seeing the bees, scattered the hay about. Of course the bees were upon him in an instant, and stung him all over his face and hands. This induced him to curse furiously at me again for not having warned him; but I quietly remonstrated that the bees were stinging him so for his wicked blaspheming, as I had passed those same bees and they had not molested me in the least.

After the third week the farmer ordered me to leave, as he did not require my services any longer. I was willing to go, but demanded my pay. This he refused to give me until I threatened to go to law about it. Then he wished me to continue. I did so until the end of the month, when he gave me twelve dollars and offered fifteen dollars for the following month, but I had quite enough of this and answered, "No, I would not work for you any longer for fifty dollars a month." I left him immediately and returned to New York City. In New York I went to Rev. A. G. Ruliffson, at 105 East Seventeenth Street, who was an intimate friend of Dr. Shadd, missionary in Persia, and who was at the head of an institution where ladies prepare themselves for missionary work.

While stopping here I was studying the language, and at the same time doing odd work around the premises. Rev. Ruliffson wrote to the president of a college at River Plains, N. Y., and asked him if he could do something to help me get an education. The following is his reply:

RIVER PLAINS, N. Y., Sept 15, 1890.

DEAR BRO. RULIFFSON:

I have conferred with some of the good people here, and we have come to this conclusion with reference to Isaac Adams. We will try to educate him, getting what help we can from various sources. We have some missionary money coming in here, the Presbytery may help and his own church in Orange may help. We will keep him until January 1st next, anyhow, expecting to keep him longer, of course.

We hope by that time that the way will be clear where the funds are to come from to keep him going. By that time the church will be well acquainted with him, which will help, no doubt. Have him come right on, and if all is well he will have a home with me as long as he wants to go to a secondary school. If he takes the 4 p. m. train, via Dutchess Junction, he will be here at 7:30. If he takes the 8 a. m. train, via Dutchess Junction, he will be here about noon.

The sooner he gets here the better, as we began school last week.   Fraternally yours,

A MATTICE.

Mr. B. W. Tice, superintendent of the West Side Boys' Lodging House of the Children's Aid Society, wrote a letter to Gen. Armstrong for admission to the

Hampton Normal Institution, of which Gen. Armstrong was principal, and the answer was favorable; so there were two places open for me to attend school.

But after considering the matter, and also meeting Gen. Armstrong, I decided to go to Virginia.

Here I worked in the mornings at the tailor's trade, and in the afternoon and evening I went to the night school, where I enjoyed my work and am much indebted to the teachers and all connected with the schools for their help and kindness shown towards me.

While here I received a letter from Kasha Sayad, of Persia, stating that the house or church in which they were worshipping was taken by the authorities and given to the people who belonged to the Nestorian Church, and who did not belong to the Evangelical Church; and I translated the letter and sent it to the Presbyterian Foreign Mission Board, in New York, as Kasha Sayad had also requested me in that letter to do all I could for them in stating the matter before such as loved the cause, and try to raise funds for erecting a house of worship for them.

I also wrote a letter to Mr. W. A. Shadd, a missionary who was at this time taking his theological course at Princeton, and received the following reply:

14 OLD SEMINARY,
PRINCETON, N. J., January 21, 1891.

DEAR FRIEND: Your letter came yesterday. I was very glad to hear from you, and also that your interests in Persia and your native village is still active and earnest I am sure anything you can do to raise funds for a new church in Wazerawa will be very much appreciated. The need there is great and the people are very poor. The old church is not suited to gatherings for preaching services; it is so damp and dark, and, besides, its possession by the Evangelical party seems to involve them in endless litigation.

A new church building would be a great advantage to the village.

I hope you are enjoying your work and profiting much by it. Of course, if you get any money for the church building, you will send it to the mission house in New York, or direct to the missionaries in Oroomiah.

Yours very truly,

W. A. SHADD.

Dr. Mitchell had also written written to Mr. Shadd, and had enclosed my letter. The following was the reply to Dr. Mitchell:

PRINCETON, N. J., January 28, 1891.

DEAR DR. MITCHELL: I received, this evening, your note with the enclosures from Hampton, which I return with this. I thought that I had something, in some of my letters, bearing directly on this matter, but am unable to lay my hands on anything now. However, I know that in the main the facts are as Pastor Sayad represents them. Paster Sayad is the oldest of the Evangelical pastors, and is a man of very high character. The congregation is very poor, indeed, though quite large. In the past they have worshiped in the old Nestorian village church and have done much to repair and improve it. The occupancy of the old church has several times been the occasion of troubles, both with the Neftorian Bishops, incited by the English missionaries, and with the Persian authorities. A church building of their own would certainly be a great help to them, and, coming from a source outside the regular contribution to the Board, would be a very suitable object for aid, I should think.

Yours respectfully,

W. A. SHADD.

So these circumstances led me to come to New York during the summer vacation. I was cordially received by Dr. Mitchell. After the matter of the church was fully agreed upon the doctor wished me to stay, and said he would help me to go to another school, under his care.

The following is one of his recommendations:

53 FIFTH AVENUE.

NEW YORK, August 31, 1891.

It gives me great pleasure to say that I have known Mr. Isaac Adams for several months, he having been introduced to me by his instructor at Hampton Institute, Hampton, Va., and also, more fully, by our own Presbyterian missionaries in Oroomiah, Persia. At Oroomiah Mr. Adams was a pupil in the mission college and was known by the missionaries as a member and officer in the Evangelical Church in that place. Mr. Adams is in this country with the intention of fitting himself, by study, for Christian labor among his former co-religionists in Persia and Caucasus. He has been for a time a member of my own household, studying also under my direction, and I have learned to confide in him as a Christian man, and to thoroughly respect him for the steadfastness of his purpose, his fidelity to his friends and benefactors, and his industry and ability. It is unusual for me to place letters like this in the hands of foreigners from our mission fields, as I feel that I am often but imperfectly acquainted with them, but in this case I have no hesitation in departing from my rule. It is my hope that Mr. Adams will fully succeed in securing the education he seeks, and will return to labor for Christ in Persia.

ARTHUR MITCHELL, D. D.
Secretary Presbyterian Board Foreign Missions.

Then he sent me to Mr. Moody's school, at Chicago, where he paid my whole expense.

The following is a letter of Dr. Shadd which I received at Moody's school, in Chicago.

THE COLLEGE,
OROOMIAH, August 8, 1891.

MY DEAR BROTHER: Your letters to me and Mrs. Shadd have been received with much pleasure, and I have intended to write you. Mrs. Shadd wrote you once. You will sorrow with us all in the death of the beloved Kasha Sayad He entered into rest August 5th. He was as well as usual three weeks ago, but a disease attacked him (abscess of the liver) and he rapidly failed in strength. He was glad to go and be with Christ. When too weak to speak aloud he whispered, "His grace is sufficient." The funeral was on Thursday, August 6th, attended by many people. Our fervent prayer was that the spirit of Kasha Sayad may rest upon the young men. May you have it in rich measure. As to the church building, you have consulted with my son William, at Princeton, and with Dr. Laborn The expense needed is $500 or $600. If you can obtain this sum, and send it to the care of the missionaries, we will use it directly for Wazerawa church. It is very much needed, but not so much as '800 tomans.

I enclose a report of our Missionary Union. The greatest need is the truly consecrated young man to enter the gospel work. All for Christ and Christ for all is the motto of our Union. Would you like to join us and prepare to extend the blessed gospel of Christ to the great multitude who know him not? I am very glad that you are at work at Hampton. May God bless you and help you to do great service in the cause of Christ.

Yours very truly,

J. H. SHEDD.

I tried very hard to get the money for the building of the church by speaking and lecturing, but this was very difficult as I could not speak the language very plainly as yet, therefore, I left this matter entirely in the hands of Dr. Mitchell, to whom I am much indebted for his great help in this matter.

After this I tried to support myself and wrote to Dr. Mitchell about it. He said I could do so, but such expenses as I could not meet he would cover. But from 1892 on I succeeded in paying all my bills, but the doctor had spent several hundred dollars towards my support. At one time I told him I wished to pay it back, but he said: "I have not done it for your, but for Christ's sake, and, therefore, I would always be glad to hear of your success."

I also spent one year at the Garret Biblical Institute, at Evanston, Ill. While here I met Mr. A. T. Wilkinson, a fellow student from Brantford, Can., and who ever since has been an intimate friend.

In the summer of 1892, he asked me to go with him and speak in churches in Canada, which I did, he arranging the meetings for me.

The Brantford Courier of August 15, 1892, reads thus:

At the Wickliffe Hall last evening, Mr Isaac Adams, a native of Persia, gave a very interesting address. This address was Mr. Adams' last one in Canada, as he leaves for New York today, where he will stay one week and then proceed to Chicago.

ISAAC ADAMS.

SCHOOL AT KOOM.

Mr. Adams has been in Canada only forty-five days, and during that time he has given forty-three lectures on Persia, its religion, customs, etc. He expresses himself as highly delighted with his visit in Brantford, and with the kind manner in which he has been entertained during his stay here. A number of Persian curiosities were exhibited and were fully described by Mr Adams to all who wished to see them.

While in this country I wrote to my home continually, and was glad to hear that my brothers were converted; so I offered to pay their expenses to this country if they would prepare themselves for missionary work, to which they consented. But owing to the cholera their journey was delayed for a while, but at last, in 1893, they succeeded in coming to this country. Three of my brothers Abraham, David and Jacob, together with a young man named Paul John, who was 13 years of age and who was brother-in-law to my brother, came to this country.* After I had remained here five years, and studied in different institutions and lectured throughout the United States and Canada (see testimonials), and also saw my brothers admitted to different institutions, I deemed it necessary to go back to Persia and preach the Gospel to those whom I loved.

When at Patterson, N. J., where I had spoken on Sunday, I was on Monday introduced to two gentlemen from Kampen, Netherlands, who were taking a post-graduating course at Princeton. These gentlemen were Messrs. Smidt and Wielenga. Our short travel from Paterson to New York was very pleasant, and Mr. G. Wielenga said that he did not know what it was to be a stranger in a strange country until after he came to America. Therefore he urged me to visit his parents and the school at Kampen, Netherlands, on my way to Persia. He also gave me a letter of introduction.

During my five years stay in this country I had sold 4,500 pictures of myself throughout the United States and Canada.

C

On my departure I had a draft for $900 with me and $100 in cash. I left New York November 7, 1894, on the steamer City of Paris for Southampton.

I reached London November 14, and here I spent one day and went to the British Bible Society, etc.

On November 17th I reached Kampen, Netherlands. I found my way to Professor Wielenga's house, where I was cordially welcomed. I was requested to speak that very night to the students of the Theological Seminary. The following letter will explain my short visit in the Netherlands. This letter was written by Rev. B. Wielenga, a brother of G. Wielenga, to the public in America:

While I am writing these lines, our dear friend Adams has probably approached the Caucasus Mountains, and is nearer to his native country than to us. His coming and staying in our midst, and also his departure from us, has been as a passing dream, but a dream that has left a refreshing influence. An influence not only felt at my home, where he staid, but also by several churches in our country, and by thousands who heard his simple, touching words.

His arrival was unexpected and therefore the more surprising. His agreeableness and sincerity, and the many cordial letters of introduction from several of our ministers, soon made him very intimate with us. And when, at the request of the faculty, he addressed us in the chapel of our school and told us of the dark night that prevails in Persia, and of his intention to bring it the light of the Gospel, then our hearts all beat with sympathy for him and his work. We admired his courage. At the close of his address we all gathered around him to press his hand and to wish him God-speed. Professor Bavinck in turn addressed him, and assured him of our support and intercession. I still imagine Brother Adams, dressed in his rich Persian costume, among us, as he gained our sympathy by his friendly smile and courtesy.

At the request of the president, Dr. Bavinck, he again spoke to us on the manners and customs of his people. Mr. Aelders translated the words and also succeeded in giving us the sentiments of Mr. Adams. It was no surprise that the consistory of our congregation should allow him to speak in the church on Sunday evening.

The short sketch of his personal experiences, the vivid presentation of the misery in which Persia has sunken, but especially the words spoken on 2 Cor. 8:5, made a deep impression on the people, and assured us that there will be many prayers offered for Persia and the heathen world. During the week Mr. Adams again spoke in one of our halls, where many of all classes and religious beliefs attentively listened to him.

The remainder of the time the Persian missionary stayed with us, he visited the provinces of Holland and Zeeland, where he spoke in the principal cities. I would simply repeat the same thing over again if I should follow him step by step, for everywhere he received the same token of love and cordiality. Everywhere open homes, open purses and open hearts. Mr. Adams has a rare tact of making himself at home among strangers ; by his artless manner he soon becomes intimate. Probably this is because he has visited so many places in America, has been introduced in so various circles and been so heartily received by a multitude of friends. He is well accustomed to the platform and knows how to hold his audience.

The fishermen of Scheveningen he addressed differently from the educated audiences of the capital and the plainer people of Maassluis from those of busy Rotterdam ; but the result was the same. Because I had many friends in the province of Holland. I had the privilege of accompanying and introducing Mr. Adams. * * * * * * * Also among our pastors his reception was hearty. Rev. Proosdy introduced him in Leiden and Rev. Donner, the missionary director, exhorted the congregation to prayer. In the Hague, Scheveningen, Maassluis, Rotterdam, Amsterdam and Zwolle he was everywhere cheerfully introduced. In many other places large crowds assembled to hear the Persian missionary. Many tears were shed and much compassion and sympathy expressed.

On the 11th of December, I accompanied Mr. Adams to Zutfen, where he parted from us to go to Berlin in the evening.

Calm and courageous, in peaceful reliance on his God, he approached his difficult task. Although he was well aware that his life is threatened on every hand in his native country, trusting on the Lord his God he began his journey, knowing that with Him he can press through a band of robbers and jump over a wall. Gladly would we have had him remain with us still longer. His stay was very short and everything hurried. But—and this conviction we respect—the Persian people are in need of the Gospel ; their souls are in prison. He told us that if God spared him we might expect him in 1896, when he would return to America in company with two or three of his countrymen. We believe that God is with Mr. Adams, and that through him He will glorify His name.

I said Mr Adams varied his style to suit his audience, but I must add that it had everywhere the same tone of child-like reliance on God, of an honest, strong faith, and a deep conviction of his own weakness.

His request that the Americans should pray for him will surely find a hearing. Many of our people are interceding for him, that is sure.

Great treasures he did not receive from our poor people, but there were given him many mites like unto that offered by the widow of old. Several poor children brought their savings to him at our home, and many needy women took pleasure in giving a trifle to his work. Such gifts God will bless.

May God spare the life of Mr. Adams and grant that his work be blessed ; may He use him for the coming of His kingdom and the glory of His name—then will our prayers be answered.

My hearty salutation,

B. WIELENGA.

Kampen, Dec. 17, '94.

While in the Netherlands I received about $300 in collections and gifts. And also the Lord has given me since many warm-hearted friends, and no words can express my gratitude to the friends and professors in the Netherlands.

From the Netherlands I went to Berlin, Germany, where I was glad to meet my friend Mr. Schmidt, who had paid my fare from Berlin to New York in 1889. He was delighted to see me and to learn of my success, but the difficulty was that I could not speak German and he could not speak English. So we had to find an interpreter and we called on the American ambassador at Berlin, through whose kindness we were able to have a conversation. At the same time I spoke about countersigning my passport, and, after the ambassador learned my name, he said, "It is a pity your name is Isaac Adams, as it sounds like a Jewish name, and no Jews are allowed to pass through Russia." He wrote me a special letter, and another man and Mr. Schmidt went with me to the Russian ambassador, and, at last, through a good deal of talking and explanation, he countersigned my passport.

The following day Mr. Schmidt bought my ticket from Berlin to Alexandrowa, and he also gave me some money. Then I took the train for Alexandrowa; from there I bought my ticket to Valadikokas.

One evening I had to stop over in a village to change cars, but, as I had some money with me, I did not wish to go to any hotel, and I staid in the station, which was very large and had all kinds of accommodations. At about 10 o'clock all was quiet and the lights were out, and I fell asleep in a chair. As I awoke and saw nobody, I became afraid and tried to get out, but every door was locked. At about half past three in the morning I saw a man come who opened the doors and lighted the lamp, and then brought in some images and put them upon a platform. A crowd of men came in and bowed down before these images and kissed them and went through all kinds of ceremonies. All this time I was awake, but appeared to be sleeping. After a while I also stood up, and they came and asked me why I did not bow before the images and kiss the cross, etc. I told them I did not believe in it. Upon hearing this they became very angry and wanted to punish me, but very soon my train came and I went on to Valadikokas. Here I rested a few days and had the privilege of preaching several times. At about 4 o'clock in the afternoon I saw a multitude of people passing along the street. I inquired what it meant, and was told that they had an image of Holy Mary and took it to the houses to bless the people. Some have to pay a large sum of money to have the image brought into the house as they are wicked and Holy Mary will not wish to be taken into these wicked houses; therefore, they have to pay in order to be equal with the good people, and in some instances the men carrying the image will pass by the house and will say Mother Mary does not want to go into that house as the people are wicked.

From here I started for Tifflis on a four days' journey, but I took a much faster way, namely, I took a carriage from Tifflis, which was driven by fast mail horses and every two hours, or when we had passed over fifteen or twenty miles, the horses and driver would be changed. I made the journey, traveling day and night, in twenty-four hours.

In Tifflis I also had the privilege of meeting some Nestorians, with whom I was glad to speak concerning their welfare and salvation through Jesus Christ; and many people came to see me, some living thirty miles away, and they wanted me to stay and preach among them. Even after being in America again I received letters from them asking me to come, saying they would get me the permission to do so from the government.

I left Tifflis for Erivan. Here my passport was taken and countersigned, as in former cities. And here also I met two Mohammedan Sayids, who were returning to Persia, and we traveled together and spoke over many subjects, especially religion. On this journey from Erivan to Aras, the Persian frontier, we came across a number of corpses lying on the roadside, where the robbers had left them after plundering and killing them. But we were not molested as we traveled with mail horses and also the government mail and two soldiers.

At last we reached the Persian frontier, where our passports were looked over and returned to us. Here the Sayids left me.

While my passport was being examined in the government office, I spoke in a very broken Persian language, so as to make them believe that I was a foreigner, as my passport showed me to be.

I asked the officers if the roads were dangerous. They said they were, and I asked them to let me have a man to go with me. They replied that it was very dangerous to travel with one man alone, and offered to give me two men as an escort. So the two men traveled with me, and at the same time I met four Armenians who begged leave to join us. I gladly complied with their request. The first night we stopped at a village where nearly all the inhabitants were thieves and robbers.

During all this time I feigned to be a foreigner, and even the Armenians did not recognize me as being a Persian. After supper I stepped out of doors and there overheard some men making plans to kill the four Armenians; but they were afraid to do so on my account, thinking that I was a foreigner. During that night I had a soldier on each side of me, resting his gun on my body and protecting me in this manner, and the four Armenians were also very near to me.

All went well, but a few things were stolen, and in the morning we continued our journey. Toward evening of that day we came to a river, and while fording it the two soldiers, who were supposed to protect me, pointed their guns at me and demanded money; at this I immediately grasped my two revolvers which I had with me and pointed them at the soldiers; then they said they were only joking, and I told them to walk on ahead, which they did. The revolvers I had with me were not loaded, but at the next station I loaded them.

After two more days journey we reached Khoi, where the two soldiers left me. I now decided to travel with mail horses again; that is, we changed horses every two hours, and journeyed on more rapidly.

But when I reached the next village, I was so sore and stiff from constantly riding horse-back that I decided to remain here for a few days and give up horse-back riding, namely, this fast way of horse-back riding. From here I telegraphed to Oroomiah and advised my friends of my coming. After a few days, I hired some other horses and went slower. From this village I left for Gavelan.

In Gavelan I met my brother Joseph, with some friends and relatives who had come to meet me. So we, about forty in number, journeyed together and reached Oroomiah on the following day. I was glad to see many of my friends and acquaintances. But one of the saddest things for me was the death of my mother, which had occurred during my absence. But I hope and believe that she died a Christian death, as her last words were, "All my hopes are in Jesus." Thanks be to God for the blessed hope that we may meet again in the world of immortality.

After a few days rest at home and waiting upon many callers, I started out to visit my friends and those who had visited me.

As I went through the city and the villages, I found that there was great need for the blessed Gospel. I conversed with the people and on Sunday I preached in different villages and at different houses.

The people of Borashan, a neighboring village, came and asked me to establish a Christian school in their village. They also went to the lord of the village and asked his permission, and then presented me a list containing all the names of the inhabitants of the village, except one family. The lord said if this one family did not submit to this they would have to leave, and then they submitted and I established a school there.

The Roman Catholics had about twenty-five years ago established there a mission, and of course they did not like to see me endeavoring to open a school right there. They tried all they could to knock me out and bribed the Persian authorities to destroy my work, but all their attempts were in vain and today almost all the people are heartily rejoicing in the progress of our good work. I found also a very good helper, who visited continually the people of Borashan and Sanger, also Eriava, so I employed him as a teacher and helper while I was visiting the other places; and finally I was able to find some helpers who had been educated somewhat by the English and Presbyterian missionaries. When they came to me I gave them some Biblical instructions and then placed them at the head of some of these schools, and paid them a small salary. So the work continued nicely, and I spent my time visiting the schools and encouraging the teachers and expounding the Word of God.

All the expense of such a school, including fuel, school books, room rent, teacher's salary, etc., will not exceed ten dollars a month. My expense of each school has very seldom exceeded five dollars a month.

Mar Shimmon, the civil and spiritual head of the Nestorians, resides in the village of Kochanues, in the mountains of Kurdistan. He is the spiritual overseer of all the Nestorian churches of Persia and Kurdistan. Once a year he sends one of his relatives to visit the churches of Oroomiah, for the purpose of receiving the contributions of the brethren, and also to inquire as to the condition of the church itself, and any matters in question are laid before him by the bishop and priests. When I arrived at Oroomiah his step-brother was there, who became very friendly to me, but died within two months after.

On May 29, 1895, I left Oroomiah, in order to pay a visit to the Patriarch, the object of which was to have an interview with him, in order to get his permission to work among his people as all the other missionaries do. A second object was evangelistic work among the Kurds and Nestorians. After two hours of riding on the plain, we came to Anhar, a village in the mountains. Here we were told we would be killed by the Kurd robbers and murderers if we should continue our journey. We had now to decide what to do —to go on or return home. Finally, trusting in the Lord, we decided to go on. For almost four hours we rode at a gallop, fearing an attack by the Kurds. We arrived at Mavana, however, where we spent the night. The next morning a discouraging report came that the roads were in a bad condition, and that several had been killed two days previous. Nevertheless, trusting in the Lord, I continued with my servant, and after a few hours journey we reached the Turkish frontier. Here I was stopped and told I could not pass. With the aid of a little gold, judiciously administered, I overcame this difficulty.

I arrived at Marbeeshoo about 9 o'clock in the evening. This is a large Nestorian village, which contains a church 850 years old, built of very thick stones and having a very heavy stone door about three feet and six inches high. The next morning I continued on my journey and reached Dizza about 6 o'clock in the evening. Immediately after our arrival the police came and ordered me to give an account of myself. I showed him my American passport and told him where I intended to go. The police were not satisfied with this, however, and after investigating our baggage, even our clothing, he took our passport and went to the Kaimakam (the vice governor). Afterwards a few Zaptiehs (constables) came to guide us to the city, and we were told that the Mutassarif, or governor, was telegraphed to about our arrival and we would have to wait there until an answer was received. The next morning the reply came back from Valy Pasha, the ruler at Van, to detain the travelers until advice was obtained from Constantinople. Upon this the authorities at Dizza placed me in confinement, under the charge of being a spy sent out by the United States and also on my way to the Patriarch to stir him up against the Turkish government. The prison was kept guarded by two soldiers. Meantime, I was afraid they would put me to death, so I wrote a letter addressed to my brother in Oroomiah, in which I wrote the number of my passport and my citizenship paper, and asked him to telegraph the United States Ambassador at Teheran. This letter I gave to my servant, asking him to bribe a man to carry this message, and also telling him to have him put the message into a loaf of bread, of which he took several.

I was in terrible torment every hour of the day. I was in mortal terror, and expected to be put to death at almost any minute. The messenger, after being stopped and searched several times and forced to give up all his bread but one precious loaf, which contained the message, at last delivered the message to my brother. In the letter I made an agreement with the messenger that, if he succeeded in reaching my brother in two days, he should receive a large sum of money. If it would take him three days he was to get less, and if four days, still less. Consequently, the messenger hurried and succeeded in delivering the message in two days. My brother had immediately telegraphed to the American Ambassador at Teheran. Various means were instituted to secure my release, through the good offices of the United States and the kindness of the English counsellor at Tabriz and at Van. The police at Dizza first denied that any such person was confined, but finding that the case had gained such publicity, and fearing trouble, they quietly released me. In the meantime, I was kept in prison.

The following, clipped from the "Banner of Truth," a religious periodical published in the United States, has some bearing upon this matter:

ISAAC ADAMS' ARREST.

Mr. Isaac Adams, of Persia, who has given us some outline of his work among his own people, was arrested while on a journey with his servant and thrown into prison by the Governor of a Turkish province. Information of this was sent by Rev. M. Bagidararisian, a fellow missionary laboring in Urmi, in the interest of the disciples of Christ. He expresses grave fears as to the fate of Mr. Adams and requests us to urge the United States Government to use its good offices for his release. Our minister at Constantinople has communicated with the Turkish office of foreign affairs, and they disclaim and deny all knowledge of the arrest. But knowing the bitter feeling against Chistianity, and especially against native converts, we would call upon all concerned in the welfare of Christianity to carry this to the throne of grace and pray God, who has all men's hearts in His hand, to deliver him from the mouth of the Turkish lion.

The following is the copy of the communication from the State Department respecting it:

DEPARTMENT OF STATE,
WASHINGTON, July 16, 1895.

REV. JOHN C. VOORHIS,
Hackensach, N. J.

SIR: I have to acknowledge the receipt of your letter of the 12th inst., requesting the good offices of this department to secure the release of Rev. Isaac Adams, an American missionary, who is said to have been arrested by the Turkish authorities at Dizza Gavar.

This case has already been acted upon by this department on a telegram from the United States Minister at Teheran. On June 11th our minister at Constantinople was telegraphed to protest against arrest and to demand prompt orders to local Governor for Mr. Adams' release. A telegram from Mr. Terrell, dated the 11th of the present month, states that he is informed by the Minister for Foreign Affairs that Mr. Adams has not been arrested at Dizza Gavar. and that he is not in the village of Kotchannes. I am, sir, Your obedient servant,

ALVEY A. ADEE,
Acting Secretary.

My servant, however, stood by me loyally and did me excellent service, by using a careful scheme of sending letters to my brother and the Patriarch, whose residence was at Kochanues. I, on the contrary, had given up all hope of living any longer; day and night tears were in my eyes, and my cry was for the lost condition of my people. I was always praying that the Lord might spare me for a few years more, that I might see my brothers take charge of my work. Through the grace and mercy of Christ I can say, I was ready to die any manner of death, in the faith of One who thus loved us and gave Himself to die even the death of the cross for us undone sinners.

But what a joy it was to me when the doors of the prison were opened and I was once more freed from that awful torture (as they had received orders to let me go on), my language fails me to describe.

I started again next morning with my good servant and three Turkish soldiers on my way to the Patriarch. After a day's journey we came to Kermi, where there were only four Nestorian houses; there we met sixteen Kurds sitting on a flat roof, smoking pipes. When I passed by them I heard them say, "There is a man we will kill tonight and take his valuables." I went to a Nestorian house to spend the night. It being so hot, I wished to sleep on the roof, but they feared that those Kurds would come to kill me and advised me to remain indoors and hide, and I listened to their entreaties and went into a large square house, one side of which was a stable and the other side a hay and straw loft. In the other end of the building the people about thirty in number, men and women lived. They put me under the hay. For about two hours I was there, when I was nearly suffocated. I cried for mercy and they pulled me out from under the hay, and I told them if it was God's will that I should be killed, then I was ready to die. About a half-hour later I saw two Kurds approach, while I was trembling and shaking all over. I tried to appear pleasant when I saw them. The first thing they told me after they kneeled down was, that they had come to kill me and take all my valuables. I told them that I was not afraid of dying, but I impressed upon their minds that my name and former case had gained such publicity that if they should kill me the Turkish authorities would be compelled by the United States Government to give account of my whereabouts, and then the Sultan would send soldiers to massacre them and all their families in this community, and so they had better not do it. They decided so. They asked me for some sugar, as one of their number had fallen from his horse and broken his leg. I gave them some and they left me unhurt, but warned me that they were going the same way with me next morning. I could not sleep all night, and after having set out for Kochanues next morning we were soon overtaken by the Kurds of the previous ill acquaintance. We rode on together with them for a long while, until we arrived at a village closed in on two sides by high mountains. Here the leader of the Kurds halted, drew his sword, and holding it across my neck threatened to sever my head from my body instantly, unless I gave him some money. I felt the sharp edge of the sword on my coat-collar, and had my horse taken but one more step at that moment, I have no doubt but I would have had my head cut off. I quickly ordered my servant to give him money, upon receiving which he put back his sword and allowed me to ride on. Soon after this the Kurds left us, and five hours later we reached Kochanues.

From a distance we noticed a multitude before the entrance to the Patriarch's residence, and upon drawing nearer we saw that there were at least 400 persons lingering there and smoking pipes. On inquiring into the cause of this gathering, we were informed that all these people had come to condole with him on the decease of his step-brother.

— 46

The Patriarch was immediately advised of my arrival. He had telegraphed several times to the Turkish government about me, and had been expecting me for some time. Our horses were taken care of, a special room was given us and a servant ordered to entertain us and see that we were well provided for. I hastened to pay my respects to the Patriarch, and after having been ushered into his presence kissed his hand, according to the general custom. He graciously motioned to me to be seated, whereupon he opened the conversation. Upon learning the purpose that had brought me hither, to work for the good of his people, he was very much delighted.

The sixteen Kurds who had given us so much trouble on our way to the Patriarch had also arrived by this time. I had advised the Patriarch of what had happened on the way, and after having come in and paid their respects to him, he ordered them in a stern tone to go to the office. Here their fire-arms were taken from them and they were informed that they would all be punished for their evil conduct. But quite a large number of Nestorians approached the Patriarch and interceded in behalf of the Kurds, and these latter kneeled down, kissed the mat upon which the Patriarch rested and apologized for what they had done. When night came they were ordered to go to a neighboring house for lodgings; but they unanimously cried out they would not leave the Patriarch's roof, for fear of all being killed by the Nestorians. Upon this they were allowed to remain, and shown into a separate apartment, where they all passed the night together. Their object in visiting the Patriarch was to have a blood-price established for the slaying of the wife of one of their number, who had been killed in a combat between Kurds and Nestorians. The sad affair had been brought about as follows:

47

Younan Bar Malekkambar, a young Nestorian, was married and his bride was being carried by the bridal procession, when suddenly a party of Kurds came in upon them and demanded some money. In place of complying with their request the Nestorians assumed a defiant attitude; a quarrel ensued, and finally some one opened fire. Kurdish women are known always to take a prominent part in an action of this nature, and so it was also in this case. Many on both sides of the combating parties were wounded and one Kurdish woman was killed. For the death of this woman, these sixteen Kurds sought redress, and demanded of the Patriarch the privilege of putting to death Younan Bar Malekkambar, whom they pointed out as having been the originator of the whole affair. The Patriarch, however, refused to deliver Younan Bar Malekkambar into their hands, but offered a ransom consisting of sixty silver magdiah, two pieces of musketry, four mules and fifty sheep. This ransom was not considered sufficient by the Kurds, and they left dissatisfied.

In the year 1896, the Nestorian bishop, Mar Gabriel, of Oroomiah, several other prominent Nestorian clergymen, with their servants (among whom were a number of my best helpers, and Younan Bar Malekkambar), visited the Nestorian Patriarch. On their way home they were attacked by the Kurds and massacred; Younan Bar Malekkambar's body was hacked to pieces and the pieces scattered in all directions. Thus they avenged the death of that woman, as they always will take revenge for the violent death of any one of their number,' and should it take them fifty years to do it.

One hundred persons, more or less, are guests of the Patriarch every day. Each is kindly received, housed and entertained, and his horses or mules stabled and cared for. Sheep and fowls are being continually slaughtered to provide for the table, as four or five

ISAAC ADAMS.   JACOB ADAMS.   ABRAHAM ADAMS.
DAVID ADAMS.

sheep are being daily consumed. Mules are incessantly traveling to and from Musol, Dizza and Oroomiah for provisions, bringing flour and sugar to fill the Patriarch's larders. Oxen are steadily employed in drawing sufficient quantities of hay and straw, for the accommodation of horses and mules. Naturally, the expense of continually providing for such an army of people is enormous; but the Patriarch, by virtue of his office, must keep a hospitable house, and every person, without any discrimination regarding creed or nationality, is expected to be welcomed here, and be well kept; according to his social standing, may he remain one hour or two months. To defray this enormous expense, however, each visitor must contribute something, be it victuals or clothing, fowls or sheep, money or jewels—no person dare come empty-handed. In addition to this collectors are sent our regularly to collect contributions of honey, grapes, fruit, millet, wheat, cheese, wine, etc., and free-will gifts are continually pouring in also. Besides, the Turkish government pays the Patriarch an annuity of between $1,400 and $1,500. After rising very early in the morning, as he always does, and observing his daily worship, the Patriarch enters a large apartment, or hall, where he gives audience to the people who have assembled to bring all sorts of cases before him. During my stay there I was given the privilege to witness a few of these hearings. One man complained that his daughter had been forcibly abducted; a second had his cattle stolen by the Kurds; a third had been robbed on his journey. One man narrated a sad story of a caravan, among which he had traveled. It had been attacked, from twenty to thirty persons had been killed and all the goods stolen. Two leaders of devil-worshipers petitioned for redress for having been robbed and beaten nearly to death, etc. In such and similar cases the Patriarch either sends out his

D   - 49 -

own servants to recover stolen property, in which they are often successful, or he telegraphs to the Turkish government and has the matter adjusted through them. It is, consequently, nothing very uncommon to find Turkish governors and other officials at the residence of the Nestorian Patriarch.

It is impossible to adequately picture in words the awful condition in which the Christians live in these parts, so much oppressed by the wild Kurds and the Turks. On my travels there, always accompanied by two or three Turkish soldiers, I had ample opportunity to witness the outrages which Christians must endure. Whenever we had entered an Armenian or Nestorian village, the soldiers would rush into the houses and act entirely as masters of the place. They demanded food and drink such as they preferred, and their demands must be complied with under all circumstances or they would become furious, knock down doors, break the windows, slap the inhabitants in the face, shoot the chickens and other domestic animals in the yard, and carry on in a brutal manner. At one place they shot a little child, playing in the sand, just for a joke. When once we arrived at a village, late at night, they demolished the doors which were not immediately opened at their call, compelled most of the men in the village to arise from their beds and go out and cut grass in the fields for their horses. In the meantime they themselves entered the houses, and did what they pleased with the women. At one time they entered a house while the male inhabitant was watering their horses. They found a woman, with children, lying asleep in bed. They picked up the bedding, together with the persons in it, carried all out of doors, emptied the mother and her children out into the yard, and, after taking the bed back into the house, slept on it themselves. Everywhere in the Kurdistan Mountains the dwellings of the Nestorians are of the humblest kind. Many houses (but they do not deserve that name) are built half underground on account of the extreme severity of the winters, the snow there lying five feet deep on the level. In order to keep warm during this season, people live in one compartment, together with their animals, in a state of filth that beggars description. But there is another reason for this. The winters being very long, the animals owned by these people, are solely depending upon the stock of hay laid in. This hay, as well as the animals, must be kept as near as possible, owing to lawless tribes of Kurds, who are swooping down upon them, foraging their herds, pillaging their goods and burning their hay when within their reach and unprotected. However, the extortion and oppressions by the government are feared nearly as much as the Kurds.

These soldiers are called Zaptiehs, and their functions are similar to those of the patrolmen in the United States; but there is another kind of Turkish soldiers called Hamidieh, who are a great help to the Zaptieh in oppressing the people. These will seize people at their option, and then promise to release them if they pay them the money they want; if the money is not forwarded, they will be taken to prison. Here they will be penned in a cell full of vermin and filth, with twenty-five to thirty other persons, and no water given them to drink but that which Mohammedans have used for their ablutions. The treatment which such poor persons are subjected to is most shocking (a) red hot irons are pressed against different parts of their bodies; (b) they are undressed and beaten into unconciousness; (c) a collar is thrown over their heads and they are thus dragged through the streets; (d) they are left without food or drink until starved; (e) they are forced to stand up for a long time continuously, and all kinds of filth is poured down over their heads; (f) they are forced to perform shaton toppy or devil's ring, the result of which is death; hands and feet are tightly bound, they are forced to hold their hands above their heads, whereas a severe torture is administered and an unspeakable, beastly crime committed; (g) their hair is plucked out by handfuls; (h) they are mutilated and crippled in various ways; (i) they are compelled to stand erect within a box just large enough to admit one person, but the box is beset with sharp steel points on all sides; in this box they must stand for from thirty to forty-eight hours in succession, not being permitted even to attend to the wants of nature.

When sent out to collect taxes, the Zaptiehs will demand the double amount. In a week, perhaps, they will put in an appearance a second time and demand the same amount again; if their demand is not complied with, or remonstrances are offered, they will insist upon the surrender of young women and girls in the family, to glut their brutal appetites, and if refused, punishment with tortures, often even death, is sure to follow.

A compassionate reader may learn from this that the lives and property of Christians, subjects to the Sultan, are nowhere safe in the Ottoman Empire. There is no justice for them; their lives, property and honor are ever at the mercy of the meanest Musselman who may see fit to attack either. He can never prove that he has been wronged, for his evidence against a Musselman is null and void. The sacred law of the Islam states that the murder of a Christian is not a crime. Christians are strictly prohibited from carrying arms of any kind. They are held by law to practice hospitality towards any Musselman, be he official or traveler, pasha or beggar. These unwelcome guests demand the best rooms in the house, the best kind of nourishment possible, and make free with the female members of

the house to suit themselves. The men on the other
hand are helpless, having no arms or weapons, while
their guests are generally well provided in this respect;
and should they dare to enter complaint with any of the
local authorities, they would either be beaten or cast
into prison, or even shot down on the spot.

Christians are forbidden to ride on horses; they may
use donkeys for this purpose, but must descend whenever they meet a Musselman, bow low with downcast
eye, whether the Mohammedan be a beggar and he a
nobleman, or vice versa.

But to return to the tax collectors. A year's tax is
demanded in advance. In many instances, of course,
Christians will not be able to comply with this rigid
law, and beg for time; but it is not allowed them.
Their cattle, household goods or other chattels, are taken
and offered at auction, and the neighboring Kurds, who
have been previously advised of the sale, will bid the
lowest prices possible, as Christians are not permitted
to join in the bidding. The proceeds of such auction
sales are then divided among the Kurds and the Zaptiehs. Thousands of Christians have thus been reduced
to extreme want, feeding on roots and herbs for months,
and thousands more have perished and are still perish-
ing from starvation. Though not present myself at
any of the terrible wholesale massacres of Christians, I
at one time was only thirty miles distant from one of
them. A Turkish soldier, Ahhamed, with whom I had a
conversation, boasted of having himself killed thirty
men, women and children during the shocking butchery
at Sason.

Since 1820 these defenseless Christian subjects of
the Sultan have been slain at random. In 1822, 50,000
Greek Catholics were massacred at Scio; in 1843, 18,000
Nestorians in the Khurdistan Mountains; 16,000 Mar-
onites and Syrians at Lebanon and Damascus; 10,000

Bulgarians in 1876; more than 50,000 Armenians and others in Asiatic Turkey since 1894. But what shall we say of the many thousands of women and maidens who have been captured at each of these massacres, forced into Turkish harems, and are leading a life to which death were far preferable? And the throng of children who were captured and taken or sold as slaves? And again, thousands and thousands of poor, wretched fugitives, wandering about nearly naked and without food, not knowing from day to day, where to rest their heads. Hundreds of Christian villages have been totally destroyed.

Yet all non-Mohammedans might avoid all these troubles, be they Armenians, Nestorians or Jews, if they so desired. All they need do is to renounce their faith and turn Mohammedans. It is certainly true that from the moment a Christian embraces Mohammedanism, his trouble ceases. It is not astonishing, therefore, though greatly to be deplored, that many grow weak and finally yield and take recourse to this way of ending their misery. Many have already done so, and others are preparing to follow their example. May God have mercy upon these poor fellow Christians and deliver them from the cruel sword of Mohammedanism and bring them under a Christian banner.

During my visit with the Patriarch, two Roman Catholics, a priest and a layman, came and handed the Patriarch a letter from Pope Leo XIII. It had been translated into Syriac, and in it the pope urged the Patriarch for recognition. I was given this letter to read. The Pope made the Patriarch high offers of aid and assistance if he would but recognize him. "Come unto us as a prodigal son and our arms are open to receive you." This is a sentence contained in that letter. But the Patriarch answered very sternly, "We have not, we will not and we cannot embrace Romanism, as

SCHOOL AT KARASANJOVI.

we feel that it has always been antagonistic to truth, given to the worshiping of images, and Rome has ever been the greatest enemy of the Protestants; more truly Christian blood has been shed by the Romanists than even by the Mohammedans."

After a stay of twenty-three days with the Patriarch, and having made all necessary arrangements with him concerning my work, I started on my return to Persia, escorted by two Turkish soldiers, who accompanied and guarded me, having instructions to keep me from receiving any information from the people until we reached Persia. Here they left me, after I had been for forty-five days under their surveilance. I was nearly broken down in health, owing to the many privations, hardships and sickening sights I had undergone and witnessed, and felt very much relieved when, once more at home, I perceived that my school and all the rest of my work was in a flourishing condition.

My Second Journey to America.

Very soon, however, I became convinced that the nature and extent of my work demanded another visit to the United States. I did not hesitate long, made the necessary arrangements with my helpers for conducting my schools during my absence, and left Persia a second time for America.

Some time before this I had met a Dervish, named Ismail, who had entered into religious conversation with me. He, by some means or other, had begun to entertain doubts concerning his Mohammedan religion, and, upon inquiry and further searching, had been convinced that the Islam was a false religion. He was now looking for something better. I found him to be an honest, upright man, true to his convictions, and, being urged by some Christians who knew him, and by the Nestorian bishop, Mar Gabriel, I determined to take Ismail with me to Russia, where he might enjoys religious liberty. But, before doing so, I had an agreement with him that he should try and eat bread and meat like other people. As a Dervish, true to his faith, he had become of the fanatic kind, and, as he claimed, had not partaken of any food of any kind excepting raisins, for "to let the body suffer will enrich the soul," was one of the axioms in which he believed. I myself entertained some doubts at first as to the varacity of his statements, but found them substantiated by many people who had known him for years. He had been with me for two or three months when we left Persia, and I had tried to get him accustomed to wholesome food again gradually, by mixing crumbs of bread with his raisins.

It was not an easy task, nor was it altogether safe to take a Dervish with me on my journey. I, consequently, arranged it so that Ismail traveled at night, while I and a youth, Abshallom George by name, whom I also took with me, traveled during the day. In the evening, after our arrival at some place, Ismail would meet us, and Abshallom would give him food and money and the name of the next station where he could meet us. This was a very necessary precaution on our part, as in Persia and Turkey a Dervish who renounces his faith and openly confesses Christianity is doomed. In Tabriz there was a slight commotion among the Mohammedans when some one publicly claimed he had seen a Dervish coming and going in and out where we lodged. Our host and hostess, however, contradicted him by stating that the Dervish had arrived one day sooner than we, and so the gossip was silenced. After we were safely through the Caucasus, Russia, we could allow Ismail to travel in our company, which we gladly did. It was both his and my earnest desire to get with him to Tifflis, where I expected him safe enough to remain and be baptized. But I very soon found that I was mistaken, as not long after our arrival at Tifflis the Persian consul was informed that I had converted a Dervish to the Christian faith. The consul sent his servants to investigate. I, having been warned, however, was prepared. I had a carriage waiting at the back door, and, when the servants of the consul entered the house, Abshallom, with the Dervish, left it through the back door, and in the carriage were immediately taken to the depot, where they left for Valadikokas. Nevertheless, the consul's servants had found some of the "holy instruments" of the Dervish in my apartments and had taken these with them to the consul, who, in consequence, threatened to follow the matter up more closely.

Upon this I despatched a messenger and informed the consul that, if he did not let this matter rest just where it was and have the articles his servants had taken from me speedily returned, I should certainly seek and find redress by appealing to all the rest of the consuls. This had the desired effect and I recovered my property. While in this city I also embraced the opportunity to settle my accounts with the British Bible Society, the London house having turned the matter over into the hands of their agents at Tifflis. I sent a large number of Bibles to Persia, and took a few only, and in various languages spoken in Russia, with me, as I thought I might make use of them on my journey. After several days I reached Valadikokas. where I met Abshallom with Ismail. I had entertained the idea of leaving the latter there, but here also we soon learned that among the many Mohammedans living or sojourning in this place Ismail was not safe. He also exhorted me to take him somewhere where he would not see any more Mohammedans, whatever. So I bought three tickets to Alexandrowa, via Harkow, Kiew and Warsaw. But between Rostow and Harkow I was robbed on the train and we were obliged to lay over, as I had no more money. We stopped at the depot for two days and three nights, I trying to sell my Bibles during the day. The people were Polanders, but I had only a few Polish Bibles with me. These were soon sold, as also some curiosities I had brought with me. I now bought three tickets for the next station. This was on the German frontier, and here we were detained by the officials, who claimed they could not let us go on to Germany with as little money as we had. We told them our story of having been robbed of our money in Russia, and I tried to impress upon them that I had friends in Berlin who would supply me as soon as I arrived there, but all to no avail. There remained nothing for us to do but to sell nearly everything we had (even my razor) and raise money. In this manner, with the help of God, I finally succeeded in getting all three of us to Berlin, and have still a few marks left.

In Berlin, we were taken to a mission-house, where we were cordially welcomed, and spent a few days. All this time Ismail had not abandoned his Dervish clothes and his long, waving hair. Now I entreated him to make a radical change in his exterior and turn also outwardly into a good Christian. He consented, and we forthwith took him to a barber's shop. A suit of clothes was given him to put on, and he now began to look like one of us. We had each a separate bed to sleep in. Next morning Ismail came to me grumbling and excited. He could not get along with putting on his new clothes. He had his trousers on back part in the front, his collar was upside down, his suspenders were buttoned over his coat, etc. This irritated him greatly, and he insisted upon having his own garments back and did not want these clothes any longer. I adjusted his clothing and talked to him kindly, upon which he became soothed and went with us to the breakfast table. But we were quite late and therefore alone in the dining room. For the first time in his life Ismail tried to make use of a knife and fork. His first attempts were very awkward, and I told him to watch us and then do as we did. He tried it, but stuck the fork so far into his mouth that the points pricked him. Now he grew angry, threw knife and fork upon the floor, overturned his chair and sat on the floor pouting and saying he would have nothing to do with such things any more. I softly and kindly instructed him again in the use of these things, and finally he became more pleasant again. After breakfast we went out to see the sights in the city, I explaining to my companions what we saw as we went along.

In the evening Ismail grew obstinate again. He once more demanded his own old garments, and insisted on having them. I had foreseen this, however, and had ordered them burnt, with the exception of a sheep-skin the Dervishes use to sleep upon. This I let him have. He immediately took off his collar, cuffs and coat and hurled them from him, took the sheep-skin, went out into the middle of the street and lay down on the sheep-skin. Naturally, in a few moments he was surrounded by a throng of people who stared at him and watched every movement he made. I went out and tried to get him back into the house, but not until after much urging and parleying with him, did I succeed. But into a room he would not come. He spread his sheep-skin upon the floor of the hall and lay down upon it, and there he spent the night. We offered to buy him some new clothes next day, but he would not have them, saying, "Why should we endeavor to keep this fragile body clean and neat, knowing that after death it will become a prey to the worms?"

After a few days, however, he became more obedient and supple, so that I entertained the idea of taking him with me to America. My own circumstances, however, took such a turn that this was made impossible. I consequently left him in Berlin, and have not heard from him since.

I had some Syriac manuscripts brought with me from Persia. These I sold in Berlin, and thus became enabled to buy tickets for myself and Abshallom to Hanover. Here I called at the office of the American Consul, who helped me on to Salzbergen, where I stopped at the station depot again for three nights. I had yet some German Bibles left, and a few pieces of needle-work or embroidery, and tried to sell both ; but owing to the language, of which I understood nothing, and to the fact that the inhabitants were all Roman Catholics, I could not dispose of anything, and we were both nearly starved. On one evening I set out on a lonely walk and was lost in a forest through which I wandered. I could not find my way back to the station until nearly 4 o'clock in the morning. But while wandering on and on, trying to find the depot. I crossed some fields, and was overjoyed when I noticed some turnips growing in one of them. I pulled a few and ate them, and was greatly refreshed. I did not forget, either, to take some turnips with me for Abshallom, who had been patiently waiting for me at the depot. When first he caught sight of me he cried for joy, for he had already given me up for lost, thinking I had been killed by some one or devoured by wild beasts. Upon the arrival of the first morning train, I called to the passengers leaving the train, "Is there any person who can speak English?" Immediately a young man came to me, and upon hearing what I had to say to him, directed me to Bentheim, where, he said, there was a society called "Newton." After several hours walk I came to that place, but found the people very unkind and irreligious. They said they were not able to assist us in any manner. When I left this place tears rolled down my cheeks, and I knew not what next to do, but thought we should surely have to starve.

As I was walking along the street, almost despairing, I saw a book store with some Bibles in the show window. Upon finding that the keeper could understand some English I offered him my Bibles for sale. He called me in, and, after learning my circumstances, said he had heard of me before. He fed me, and gave me some eatables also for Abshallom,* whom I had left at the depot. Besides this he presented me with ten marks, and another person, who was present and overheard our conversation, handed me three marks more. This money enabled us to go to Kampen, Netherlands, where I met my most honorable and dearly beloved professors and friends. The following letter, addressed to the Hon. Mr. Ittman, of Rotterdam, will tell of my short visit at Kampen:

MOST HONORABLE GENTLEMAN: You will undoubtedly remember Mr. Adams, who visited us in 1894. He is on his journey to America, where he hopes to be ordained as missionary. He deems this necessary, as his work has become very extensive in the schools, and as he will be better equipped.

Last Sunday a telegraph dispatch from Hanover informed us that Mr. Adams and his friend were at that place, in very critical circumstances, as they were robbed of their money in a train, in Russia. He arrived there without a penny with him, and, as we thought best he should not longer be detained here, we gave him one hundred and twelve guilders and fifty cents for his journey to America. This money was partly received formerly and partly contributions of our own.

It is necessary that he, in America, should complete his business as soon as possible and return to Persia.

If this money might not be sufficient (we do not know the price, third class,) then he will, without doubt, be sustained at your place. I can assure you that the money is perfectly well employed; we have obtained a good impression of his work through many letters and photographs.

B. WIELENGA.

At Rotterdam I called upon Mr. Ittman and some other friends, from whom I received donations as follows: Fifteen guldens of Mr. Ittman; twenty guldens from G. Van den Boom; twenty guldens from J. L. Van den Boom; ten guldens from Mr. Van den Kooi, and twenty-five guldens from the Reformed Church at Rotterdam. These friends also offered to purchase for me a second-class ticket to New York, but I declined the kind offer, saying that they might better help me along in my work.

I therefore left Rotterdam with Abshallom for New York.

The following is one of the reports of my schools since my second arrival in this country:

OROOMIAH, PERSIA.

REV. ISAAC ADAMS:

DEAR BROTHER: In my last letter I sent you the report of the school of Balaf, and also of Mart Maryam. Herewith I send you the report of the other schools:

SCHOOL OF KARALARY—NUVIA, Teacher.

He has a nice and warm room where the children are instructed.

Class 1. They have begun with the spelling book and have completed it, and also have read the Gospel of Matthew, and are up to the 15th chapter of Mark, and they are taught the history of the Old Testament, and have also committed to memory fifteen pages of the question book.

Class 2.—This class also began with the spelling book and have completed the same, and have learned the Gospel of Matthew, and also fifteen pages in the question book. This class was brave and gave good satisfaction in examination.

Class 3. They are in the spelling book up to page 10, and three pages in the question book.

Class 4.—They are all small children, who are just beginning the spelling book, and are taught the Lord's prayer.

—62

The village is in great need of this school, but it is necessary for the teacher to be faithful. There is no other school in this village, neither is there any other Christian worker. It is a grand field of labor for a faithful teacher.

SCHOOL OF MOORASCHERRY—GEWERGES, Teacher.

Class 1. They read in the New Testament in the modern Syriac language, and also Genesis in the ancient Syriac. They gave a good showing in arithmetic, in the Lord's prayer, ten commandments and apostle's creed. They also have had stories from the Old Testment, and have learned to write.

Class 2.—They began with the spelling book, have completed the same, and also the Gospel of Matthew, and are now in the Gospel of Mark.

Class 3.—They began with the spelling book, and have completed the same, and have just started in the Gospel of Luke.

Class 4.—There are six boys and girls just beginners in the spelling book.

In all the classes of this school, instruction is given in the Lord's prayer, ten commandments and apostle's creed. In this school we have three children of Mohammedans that is from the Sheah's sect, and also a Soonnees, whose name is Ali. He has learned two pages from Goolistan, and he has newly begun on the Gospel of Matthew in the Persian language. In this village there are forty-two houses ; eighteen are Nestorians and the rest are Mohammedans, and there is no other school besides this. The teacher here we found to be very faithful. Every evening he visits the houses and holds conversation about Christ with the parents of the children, and he does good work in the village. There is good testimony about him from the village. He is a worthy and faithful young man. We found him busy with his school. May the Lord bless his work. It's an excellent field for labor among Musselmen and Nestorians.

SCHOOL OF ALKAI—K. BENYAMIN, Teacher, assisted by GEWERGES, JR.

The total of pupils here at present is thirty-two; of these, fourteen are boys and eighteen are girls. One girl died with diphtheria ; she was 11 years of age. There are two others sick in bed.

Class 1 –In the ancient Syriac, the Gospel of Mark and in Genesis up to the 17th chapter In Turkish language, they have begun in the Gospel of Matthew up to the 10th chapter. In

Persian they have studied three chapters in Genesis. In arithmetic, they are up to division ; and they have a good knowledge of Bible stories, and have fine hands for writing.

Class 2.—In the ancient Syriac, they have studied nine chapters in the Gospel of Matthew. In the Turkish language they have studied forty-three pages in the spelling book. In the modern Syriac they study in Genesis.

Class 3.—In the ancient Syriac, with its translation into modern, they have begun from the 1st chapter of Matthew to the 13th. In the Turkish spelling book they are up to page 17, and have a good start in writing sentences.

Class 4—In the modern Syriac, they have begun from the 1st chapter of Matthew and are now to the 14th chapter. In Genesis, they have just begun in the modern Syriac.

IN THE GIRL'S DEPARTMENT.

Class 1 They have begun with Matthew and are up to the 6th chapter of Luke. They have studied a little in the ancient Syriac from the beginning of Matthew. They have also learned the smaller arithmetic, and have three pages in the spelling book of the Turkish language. They also have penmanship.

Class 2.— The ancient Syriac began from the first of Matthew and they are now up to the 14th chapter of Mark. They have just started to learn to write.

Class 3—They are all in the spelling book.

The most of the boys and girls in this school, except the 3d class of the girl's department, can recite the Lord's prayer and apostle's creed, and some of the higher classes can also recite the ten commandments.

The teachers are very faithful and quiet and love teaching the pupils This school is in good order, but all the work in it, we may say, is the fruit of Kasha Benyamin, who is in great anxiety for its success.

SCHOOL OF DARBARY AVRAHAM, Teacher.

Class 1—Study the New Testament up to the Gospel of John, and the Old Testament up to Exodus ; arithmetic up to subtraction : spelling up to writing of sentences.

Class 2 Fourteen boys and girls are in this class. They are all in the spelling book, and instructions are given to them in Bible stories, and they are taught the Lord's prayer, ten commandments and apostle's creed. Karram, a Mohammedan, has studied five chapters in Goolistan, and two chapters in Tarrusel,

SCHOOL AT MART MARYAM.

1. JOSEPH ADAMS.   2. MRS. JOSEPH ADAMS.
        3. KASHA OSHANA.   MRS. KASHA OSHANA.

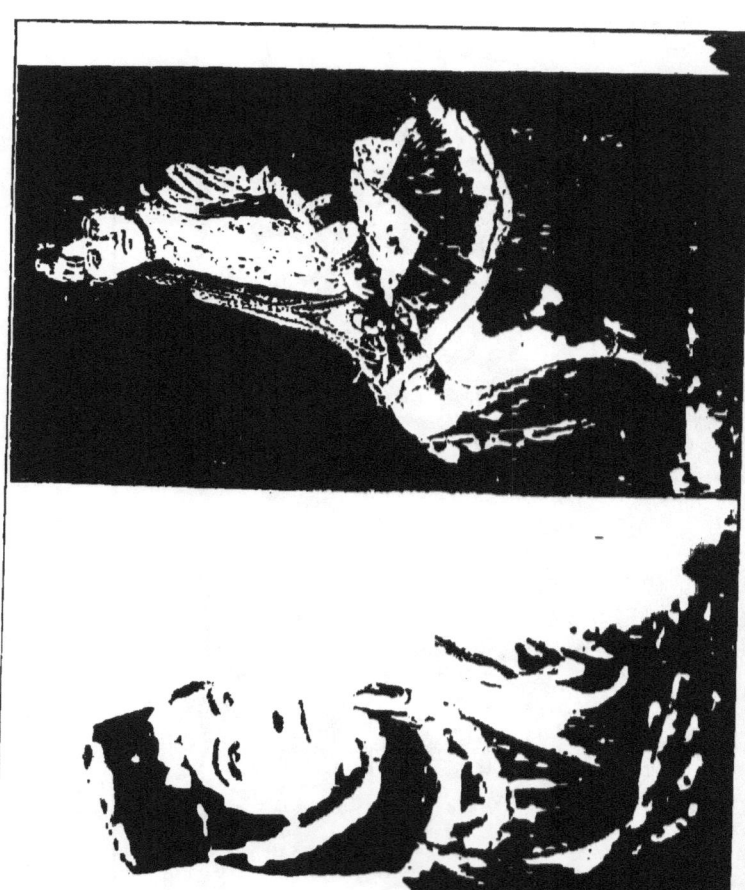

YOUNG CHRISTIAN PERSIAN LADY.

INDOOR COSTUME.

ind seven chapters from the Gospel of Matthew in the Persian anguage. In the Syriac language, he is in the speller.

The teacher does the house-to-house visitation every evening ind people are glad to receive him and listen to the Gospel stories We have had good testimony for him from the inhabiants of the village, and they are all pleased with his work and nanner of conduct. There is no other school building here besides ours. The school is not very comfortable as the roof is quite low.

SCHOOL OF KARASANLOVI, ASYAD, Teacher.

Class 1.—Completed the Gospel of Matthew and Mark, and ire now to the 14th chapter of Luke. And in Turkish language hey have studied fifteen pages in the speller, writing of words ind sentences.

Class 2.—Up to the 12th chapter of Mark. Catechetical instructions—that is, Bible stories, ten commandments, Lord's prayer, etc , are given to this and all the other classes.

Class 3 —Completed the speller, and studied thirteen pages in the book called Deaf and Dumb. They will soon begin with he Gospel of Matthew.

Class 4.—They have started the speller and have gone to the 1st page. Lord's prayer they have committed to memory.

Class 5.—There are thirteen boys and girls and are all beginners I can most heartily speak a good word for Teacher Asyad, for her care and earnestness in teaching these little ones he fear of the Lord and the spiritual catechism. The subject which they study she causes them to understand. Her aim is not only to put the truth in the heads of her pupils, but also in the heart, and she does not hesitate to teach the stories in the Bible.

This is the only school in Karasanlovi.

SCHOOL OF BORASHAN—AGASY, Teacher.

Class 1.—In the ancient Syriac, they began from the Gospel of Matthew and are up to the 24th chapter, with the translation in the Modern Syriac. And reading from the different parts of he Testament. Have completed the smaller arithmetic and started the larger one.

Class 2.- Have studied twenty-seven chapters in the Gospel of Matthew, in the modern Syriac, and two chapters in the ancient Syriac, and smaller arithmetic.

Class 3.—Began with the speller and completed the same, and have also studied six chapters in Mark.

Class 4—Started the beginning of speller and have completed the same; have studied three chapters of Mark

Class 5.—There are nine boys and girls.   They are all in the speller.

All the classes in this school, except the 4th and 5th, can recite the Lord's prayer, ten commandments and apostle's creed, while the two classes can recite the Lord's prayer only.

This is the only school in this village.

SCHOOL OF ERIAVA—K. PATROUS, Teacher.

This school had thirty-two pupils, but, because a missionary came to the village and gave alms to the poor, eight children went away to get alms There are two other schools besides our own here, —one of the Roman Catholics and one of the Presbyterians; but the number of pupils in our school exceeds both of the others.   I suppose the children who went to the other school to get alms will soon come back, that is, after the alms-giving is suspended.

Class 1.—The New Testament in the ancient Syirac has been studied with translation into that of modern.   The larger arithmetic, up to subtraction.   In the speller, up to writing words and sentences, and catechetical instruction.

Class 2.—Modern Syriac, first three Gospels, smaller arithmetic and writing.

Class 3.—Modern Syriac, begun from the first part of Matthew up to the 12th chapter ; previously they repeated the speller.

Class 4. —Began the speller and have completed it and started from the Gospel of Luke.

Class 5.—They are all small children and are just beginners.

SCHOOL OF SANGAR—ABSHALOM, Teacher.

Class 1. —Have studied Genesis, with the translation from the ancient to modern Syriac.   Have completed the question books Have studied arithmetic to subtraction, and from the Gospel they have studied ten chapters in Matthew and seventeen in Mark

Class 2.—They have studied six chapters of Genesis, with the translation from the ancient to the modern Syriac.   They are nearly through with the question book.   They have studied arithmetic to subtraction.   They have started with the Gospel of Matthew.

Class 3.—They have studied fifteen chapters in the Gospel of Luke, with translation from ancient to modern Syriac, and five chapters in Genesis, in the modern Syriac language. All these classes have also writing, and are able to repeat the Lord's prayer and ten commandments, and also have learned many passages out of the Scriptures.

Class 4.—There are eight boys and girls in this class and are all just beginners. They have just begun with the speller,

SCHOOL OF KOOM—ABRAHAM, Teacher.

Class 1.—Completed the speller and started in the Gospel of Matthew. They are up to the Gospel of Luke; of course, they simply give a repetition to the speller; small arithmetic.

Class 2.—They have just completed the speller, expect them to begin with the Gospel soon.

Class 3.—They are advanced in the speller.

Class 4.—They are all beginners Instruction in Bible stories, the Lord's prayer, ten commandments, and apostle's creed is given in this school. There are no other schools besides ours in this village. All the schools (eleven) begin between 8 and 9 o'clock in the morning.

First, after all pupils are present, leaving their shoes in the hall while keeping on their hats, the teachers read a portion of the Scriptures, after which he puts simple questions to the pupils concerning what he had read; then he opens with prayer. Then he starts from the first class, and so forth, listening to their recitations. The teacher is sitting in the center of the room, and when the class comes to recite, they form a circle around him, while the other pupils are sitting against the walls of the room, yet the pupils are allowed to ask questions at any time. The school is closed with one of the pupils reciting the Lord's prayer: that is at about 12 o'clock. School starts again at 1 o'clock and closes at 5 o'clock. The last hour, between 4 and 5 o'clock, is given entirely to Bible instructions.

Most of our schools meet on Sunday with the teachers, in like manner, for religious purposes. The pupils who are in advance will recite seven verses, anywhere out of the bible, and the others will recite one, and some just one sentence, as "God is love."

As has been stated previously, the teacher visits the homes and the parents of the children and tries to increase the attendance in the school, and speaks to the parents about the Gospel.

The field is great and the laborers are few, but let it be known to you that the work is progressing nicely and the prospects grow brighter every day. We may expect a great work in the future. We hope everything will be written to you fully, that you may know that the efforts of our friends have not been in vain. May the dear Lord reward them in his Kingdom above. Amen.   Yours truly,

                    KASHA OSHANA.
                    ESHAKAN,
                          Examiners.

This is a literal translation of the report I have received. I believe this is a statement which will make the hearts of those who have helped in my work, with their small and great donation, rejoice in the Lord with thankfulness; that through these gifts there had been planted eleven schools, children and youths are being taught not only education and civilization; but the secret knowledge of our blessed Redeemer, who loved such as these, and who said, "As much as you do unto these little ones, ye do unto me."

Surely, we may say that the Lord reigneth, and who knows but out of this humble work we may see a great opening for the proclamation of the Gospel in my country.

I deemed it necessary to send my brother Abraham to care for this work during my absence, and he, therefore, left New York October, 1897.

The following is a letter from my brother Abraham, received lately:

                  MART-MARYAN,*
          OROOMIAH, PERSIA, February 24, 1898.

DEAR BROTHER: I have just returned from Karasanlovi, whereas, I was yesterday in Alkai. I am glad that I can give you a good report concerning the schools I found also that the

---

*Two wards of Oroomiah city are inhabited by Christians. One is known by the name of Gol patali-Khan; here live the Armenians, and among them is the French mission headquarters; the other is inhabited by the Assyrians or Nestorians. American and English mission workers have their headquarters here. This part is known by the name of Mart-Maryan. The name is taken from the church erected here in the honor of the Virgin Mary. The tradition as to the erection of a church here is, that a priest, while asleep, dreamt that a woman appeared to him. He asked her name. She answered: "I am Mary, mother of Jesus; thou shalt build a church here in my name, and let all mothers, who may lack milk to nourish their children, come to my shrine, and I will make their supply plentiful." So the women, of all religions, from distant parts of the country, will come with wax candles, sheep and dove sacrifices, and also with the incense, to seek her blessing.

ignorance and superstition of the people is almost without description. The men say, woman has no part in the resurrection, and the women themselves have no knowledge of future life; but to their great surprise they have heard and hear about God's love to them, and the story of the cross seems so wonderful to them that they cannot believe it, especially that He should care for them and be their Savior.

At first there was some prejudice as to the school and the work, but now many come to hear and ask about that wonderful Savior.

Some people, more especially the older ones, have a great idea that Heaven is to be merited by strict observance of the fastings, especially at this time, as fifty days are observed before Easter. But, as you know, they abstain from meat and oily substances, but they do not cease to swear and do other wicked things. However, thanks be to God, that the power of the holy life of Christ is seen in the respect now shown them, and in the increasing readiness to hear them again and again.

At 9 o'clock the examination commenced in the school room, which was crowded by the parents and people of the village.

The pupils occupied the middle of the room. The studies in which they were examined were modern and ancient Syriac, Perian and Turkish languages, geography, spelling, arithmetic, Bible history, reading and writing. But what pleased me most was the recitations of the different verses and passages of Scripture, one child reciting a whole chapter. And in all the work the pupils did credit both to themselves and their teacher. The singing especially pleased the parents, many of whom loudly expressed their astonishment, especially at seeing that the girls as well as the boys could be educated.

The teacher not only taught them to pray, but also to love Jesus; and she is in the habit of praying with different pupils, alone, each day, and the school also is opened and closed with prayer. The teacher has also done much to interest the parents in religion.

In short, I can say that the good seed is being sown, and hope the Lord will bless the work and will strengthen the teachers to do still more for the Master.

My brother, do all you can, through the help of God, to spread the Gospel of our dear Lord to these ignorant and superstitious people.

I assure you that your struggles have not been in vain.

I am, your brother,

ABRAHAM ADAMS.

—69—

PART SECOND.

PERSIA is called Iran by the natives. It extends nine hundred miles west and east and seven hundred miles north and south. The present boundaries are: The Caspian Sea and the Transcaucasian provinces of Russia on the north; Bokhara, Afghanistan and Boloochistan on the east; the Strait of Ormuz and the Persian Gulf on the south; Asiatic Turkey on the west. It has an area of 648,000 square miles.

Many nations of whom we read in the Bible and in history have lived or had their representatives in Persia, but only one of these is in existence at the present time. We know of Egyptians, Assyrians, Babylonians, Greeks and Romans as having once been prevailing powers, mighty empires of the world; but they have either vanished from the face of the earth or their power and glory has faded away and they have dwindled into insignificant provinces of other empires and kingdoms. Persia has held its own; it still occupies the same position it did centuries ago.

It is also remarkable as a Bible-land. By many Persia is claimed as the region where the Garden of Eden was situated; where Abraham was born; where Daniel prophesied. It was under the rule of Cyrus the

Great, and the home of the wise men who were the first representatives of the gentiles who came to worship the infant born Christ.* When Assyria led the Jews captive to Babylon, it was Persia who humbled her power and vanity and restored Juda to her native land, to rebuild the house of the Lord.

Her glory, today, has flown away and her splendor has faded, but her physical beauty still remains. Persia is a paradise, intoxicating people with the fragrance of its roses. It is a garden, wreathing the faces of mankind into smiles by its beautiful streams.

The national emblem of the empire is the lion and the sun, which accounts for the fact that it is occasionally called the land of the lion and the sun.

According to Shah Nameh of Friduei the history of Persia begins some thousand years before the Christian era. The northwestern part of Persia, called Media in ancient times, was known to the Greeks as the Assyrian Empire. But the Medians under Dejoce, in 708 B. C., shook the Assyrian yoke from off their necks and subjugated the other tribes of Persia. In 538 Cyrus of Persia rebelled against the Medes, was victorious, and extended the southern frontier of his domain to the river Oxus and Indus and annexed Asia Minor, Syria, Palestine and Mesopotamia. He was succeeded by his son Cambyses (529-522), and the latter by Darius (522-521). This dynasty ruled until Darius III. was compelled by Alexander the Great to acknowledge his superiority, the latter being several times victorious over him and conquering all Persia.

Under the leadership of the tribe of Arsoude, Persia once more regained its independence in 246 B. C. But the dynasty of Arsoude came to an end at the hands of Ardasher Babajans, who managed to gain possession of

---

*According to tradition the tomb of one of the three wise men is located near my home, and a church is erected at Mart-Maryan in his honor.

more than one-half of the entire country, namely: the provinces of Fars, Kerman, and the whole of Irakiston. In 218 B. C., however, this valiant prince and warrior conquered the whole nation and was crowned "King of Kings" (Shahin Shah in Persia). This was the beginning of the famous dynasty of the Sassanidæ, under whose reign Persia acquired unprecedented power and prosperity. Their last ruler succumbed to the Arabs in 636 A. D., and these ruled Persia till 750 A. D. The tribe of the Abbosides now assumed the Persian throne, but was in turn soon overthrown. The country was thereupon divided into different provinces, until in 1253 it was conquered and subdued by the Mongols under Genghis Khan and his grandson, Khulakum Knan. The former was a Christian. During his reign Moryaw Al-aha was the Nestorian patriarch and under his care the church was very successful. The Mongol dynasty lasted until 1335 A. D.

A new dynasty arose in western Persia in 1500 A. D. Ismael, the descendant of an ancient family of devotees and saints, became the leader of a number of tribes which united under him, and with the aid of which he overturned the rule of the Turkoman and made Aderbjon his capital. His followers held him in the highest esteem on account of his personal valor and owing to the high rank of his family revered him. He rapidly subdued western Persia, and in 1511 took Kurason and Balkh from the Uzbecks. In 1514 he encountered a far more formidable enemy in the mighty Salim, Sultan of Turkey, whose zeal for the conquest was fanned by religious fanaticism having developed into hatred against the Shutes, the followers of Ishmael largely adhering to this sect, and who in turn were fiercely inflamed against the Sunites, the subjects and followers of the Sultan. In the ensuing conflict Ismael was defeated, but Salim could not record any great gain from this victory. Ismael's son, Shah Tah-masip, who reigned from 1523 to 1576, subdued all the Uzbecks of Khorazon and frequently defeated the Turks without suffering the loss of a single battle. He takes rank as a prudent and spirited ruler.

Shah, Abbas I, the Great, who was one of the most glorious of Persia's modern kings, ascended the throne in 1585 and ruled until 1628. He restored internal tranquility and repelled the invasions of the Uzbecks and Turks. In the year 1605 he gave the Turks such a terrific drubbing that they made no more trouble during his long reign. He also restored to his kingdom Kurdistan Mosul and Drarbekin, which had long been separated from Persia. Abbas' government was strict, but just and equitable. Roads, bridges, caravansories* and other conveniences for trade were constructed at great cost, and the improvement and ornamentation of the towns were not neglected. Many of his large caravansories which bear his name remain to this day.

Isphahan, his capital, in a brief period of his reign, doubled its population. His tolerance was remarkable, considering the character of his ancestors and subjects, for he encouraged the Armenian Christians to settle in the country, well knowing that their peacable, industrious habits would enhance the prosperity of his kingdom.

His successors were Shah Sufi, (1628-41), Shah Abbas II, (1641-66), and Shah Soliman, (1666-94). During the reign of Shah Sultan Hussein (1694-1722) a weak and foolish prince, priests and slaves were elevated to high

---

*King Abbas ordered one of his officers to construct 1,000 caravansoris, the cost of construction to be paid for from the king's treasury. The officer built only 999, and when the king inquired if he had finished his task, he replied that he had built one less. This made the king very angry and he ordered the officer to be beheaded. The officer requested the privilege to speak, which the king granted. Then the officer said: "Long live the king! I did this for the honor of the king, because it would take the people longer to say 999 than 1,000." This pleased the king so that he spared the officers' life and gave him a high office.

offices and the Sunnites suffered sore persecution. The result was that Afghan besieged the king in Isphahan, Hussein abdicated in favor of his conqueror, who ultimately became insane and suffered deposition in 1725 at the hands of his brother Ashrab.

The atrocious tyranny of Ashrab was suddenly checked by the celebrated Nadir-Shah. Hussein and Ashrab belonged to the dynasty of Sayides, a holy sect, descendants of their prophet Mohammed.

Nadir-Shah was one of the greatest warriors of Persia. He raised Tah-Masip (1729-32) and his son, Abbas III, (1732-36), of the Suffivian race, to the throne, and then on some frivolous pretext deposed Abbos III and seized the scepter himself (1736-47). Nadir was assassinated by Imam-Kuli-Khan, of Oroomiah, whose descendants now live very near our mission station in Oroomiah. Again after the murder of Nadir, Persia was divided into many independent states and became a field of blood. Beloochistan and Afghanistan became independent till 1755, when a Kurd, Karim Khan (1755-79) abolished this state of affairs, re-established peace and unity in western Persia, and by his justice, wisdom and warlike talents acquired both the esteem of his subjects and the respect of the neighboring states. He received the title, "Father of Persia." Karim Khan was succeeded in 1784 by Al Murad, then by Jaafor and the latter by Lutf-Ali Merza.

During Lutf-Ali's reign Mazandaran became independent under Agha Mohammed Khan, a Turkoman. Lutf-Ali Merza rushed into Mazandaron and killed all the relations of Mohammed Khan who were ruling there and took captive Agha Mohammed Khan, a boy only six years old, making him a eunuch.

This boy was of Kajar race. When he was in the harem of Lutf-Ali, he kept thinking how his cruel master murdered his father and all his relatives. When he sat on the royal rugs, he would take his revenge by cutting them. When of age, 20 or 25 years old, he eloped to his own country, Mazandaren, and joined his relations. He frequently attacked Lutf-Ali, and defeated him in 1795. He was then able to establish his throne in the southern part Mazandaran. This great Eunuch king founded the dynasty which rules today, restored the kingdom as it was under Karim-Kurd, and conquered Georgia and Kharasau. But he was assassinated May 14, 1797. His nephew, Futteli-Ali Shah, (1797-1834) engaged in three wars with Russia, and was defeated each time. As a result, he lost his territory in Armenia and a part of Persia namely, from the Caucasian Mountains to the River Aras, which now fixed the boundary between Russia and Persia.

Futteli-Ali, in his last war with Russia, in 1826, was entirely defeated. Besides losing some of his territory, he paid the sum of 18,000,000 rubles ($9,000,000) to Russia. The death of the Crown Prince Abbas Mirza (1833) seemed to give final blow to the declining fortune of Persia, as he was the only man who seriously attempted to raise his country from the state of abasement into which it had fallen.

Futteli-Ali had seven sons. One of them, Jahon-Suz-Mirza, lives today. Seven years ago he was governor in the author's city. After the death of the Crown Prince, each of the seven sons laid claim to the throne, while the father was still living. At the same time the Crown Prince Abbas-Mirza had a son named Mohammed. Futteli-Ali, when quite old and near death, by the aid of Russia, made Mohammed, his grandson, king (1834 1848).

Nayib-Ali-Saltana acted as regent during the boyhood of Mohammed. When he came to power for himself, he conceived the idea of restoring Baluchistan, Afghanistan, and a great part of Turkoman, to the

Persian dominion. He was especially anxious to take Herat, the key to India, but was resisted by England. The war was terminated in 1838.

Nasreddin (defender of his religion), the late Shah, (who was assassinated May 1, 1896), a young man 18 years old and very energetic, succeeded his father in 1848. Following his father's example, the new Shah tried to restore Afghanistan and Baluchistan, but was compelled by England to sign an agreement on January 25, 1858, by which he was bound not to interfere any longer in the internal affairs of Herat.

In 1858, he violated this treaty, and took the city of Herat. After a severe war with England, in 1857, in which his loss was 20,000 soldiers, he relinquished Herat, but added to Persia many provinces in the western part of Afghanistan and Baluchistan, and also some states in Turkoman.

He was one of the best kings of Persia. He visited Europe three times; once in 1873. He had European ideas and was a well educated man. He started a good system of postal telegraph and had 30,000 soldiers trained after European discipline. Above all he founded a beautiful college in Teheran, which is called in Persian Daralfnoon (the place of science). The present Shah, Mozuffur-uddine, was born March 25, 1853, and succeeded his father on May 1, 1896.

Persia is divided into thirteen states: Ghilon, Mazandaron, Astarabad, in the north; Aderbjon, Persian Kurdistan, Luriston, Kerman with Mogiston in the south; Irakeston, the capital state, where the king resides, being in the center. On the east lies the large estate of Khorason, which is mainly a desert.

The largest city is Fabriz, has about 200,000 inhabitants, and is also the most important commercial city.

The present population of Persia is about 10,000,000, composed of representatives of various nations. Each speaks its own language and uses its own national costume. There are about 30,000 Jews, 60,000 Armenians, 75,000 Nestorians, 675,000 Kruds, 15,000 Fire-worshipers, and the remainder are Mohammedans.

The Shah is regarded as the agent of Mohammed, and as such demands implicit obedience. The government is therefore an absolute despotism. The Shah appoints a governor for each state; this governor appoints a mayor in each city within his territory. This office is not awarded on the basis of education, ability or worthiness, but is given to the man who will pay the most money, provided his ancestry is fairly good. Many mayors of cities are related to the royal family. These offices are limited to terms of one year, but many times a mayor is removed before his time expires, subjects complaining loudly against him, or some person bidding more money for the office. When a man is appointed mayor of a city, the lords and counts of that city, accompanied by soldiers, will go three miles to meet the new official. He is greeted with discharges of artillery.

These lords ride on very fine Arabian horses with gold-bitted bridles and escort the mayor into the city. The new governor admires the fine horses of his lords, occasionally covets some fine steed among them, and before his term expires finds a way to get possession of it by helping the lord out of some trouble.

If the new mayor is a prince, all prisoners confined in the city jails are taken before him as he enters the city. This is to signify that as a member of the royal family he has authority to behead them.

The third day after a new mayor has arrived in a city it is customary for lords and counts to visit him with presents of money, golden trinkets, Arabian horses, etc. A mayor has from one hundred to three hundred servants. He pays them no salary. Some willingly enter his service for the name, some from fear, and others from choice. Most of these servants obtain a living from fines and bribes. Some of them are detailed to settle quarrels between men in some village that belongs to the city. This is their opportunity and they early learn to make the most of it.

Each officer is at the mercy of the higher officer who may take away his office or cause him to be executed at any time, without any trial, in any cruel manner he may desire.

The prisons are frequently cellars, underground, without windows, damp and invested with flies. They are seldom ventilated.

These pits, or prisons, are long and narrow and have each a heavy timber reaching across the middle, on which chains of iron are fastened to secure prisoners. The floor is made of clay and there is no means of admitting light or fresh air into these dungeons, which in consequence are full of all kinds of vermin. There is no bed or furniture. The government does not feed the inmates; their friends bring bread and throw it to them, and some of this even is sometimes picked up by the jailor and kept for his own nourishment. No men are allowed to visit the prisons, but wives or daughters may purchase this privilege by paying a fee to the jailor. The torture of prisoners is regulated according to the nature of their crimes. The common method of torture for thieves, robbers and murderers, is to put the bare foot of the criminal in a vise, and squeeze it until he cries in agony. If he gives the jailor some money, or promises to give some the next time his friends visit him, the pressure on the foot is lessened. If a man goes to jail wearing good clothes, the jailor often exchanges his own poorer suit for the good ones.

The modes of execution used by the Persian Government are still barbarous in the extreme. Male convicts are put to death either by being blown from the mouth of a canon, by having their jugular arteries severed, or by being nailed to a wall. Women are sentenced to have their heads shaved, their faces blackened, then to take a bare-back ride on a donkey through the principal streets of a city or village, and finally to be put into a bag and beaten to death. Others are executed by putting them in a nude condition into a bag full of cats, who will speedily scratch and bite them to death.

Any prince of the royal family has authority to pass the death sentence upon his subjects. When occasionally an intimate friend of the ruler is appointed governor, the king will add a knife as a present, transmitting thereby the power of passing death sentence. Every prince, mayor or governor having this authority, keeps two executioners, uniformed in scarlet and walking on before their master, whenever he promenades through the streets.

Whenever a convict is to be executed, he is taken from his prison cell handcuffed and a chain about his neck, escorted by a guard of soldiers with fixed bayonets. He has probably spent several months in his dungeon, and naturally looks haggard and worn, unclean and unshaven, his clothes hanging about him in rags. The executioner, in his scarlet uniform, walks a few steps in advance, a large sharp knife in his hand. Thus they proceed to the public square, and in presence of a crowd of eager spectators the victim is ordered to kneel down. The executioner now steps behind the convict and with a single stroke of the keen blade severs the jugular vein, and another soul takes its flight, having completed its part in life's drama. In some places criminals are executed by burying their whole body, their head only excepted, in a casket of cement; this soon will set and harden around the body, and soon cause death.

An intoxicated Mohammedan, when found on the street noisy and abusive, is arrested, a cord or twine several feet long is drawn through the dividing membrane between his nostrils, and he is led publicly along the street by the executioner. The culprit soon gets sober, and is very much ashamed. As the executioner passes along the streets with him, shop-keepers give small sums of money to the former.

Men of a very quarrelsome and combative disposition are punished by having their feet tied to a post with the bare soles upward. These are then whipped until they bleed profusely, and sometimes the nails are torn from the toes. This frequently causes the victim to swoon away, becoming entirely unconscious under this terrible maltreatment.

Christians and Jews according to Persian law are not subject to decapitation, as they are considered unclean by the Mohammedans and not sufficiently worthy of this privilege. The most severe punishment is when a prince is deprived of his eyesight. Lords and counts are executed in two ways: the Shah will send him a bottle of sherbet, which is a sweet drink, but in this instance contains a deadly poison, and which he is compelled to empty: or the governor dispatches a servant to wait upon the criminal while taking his bath, and in doing so has orders to cut the veins in the criminal's arms and cause him to bleed to death.

What a contrast in the modes of punishment and their application between Mohammedan and Christian countries! The kind of punishment inflicted on criminals in any country is truly characteristic of the prevailing religion. A religion based upon love and charity

I. ADAMS, IN NATIVE COSTUME.

PRESENT SHAH.

PERSIAN OFFICER.

OF THE PRESENT DYNASTY.

will deal with its criminals effectively, but humanely and not in a barbarous manner.

CLIMATE AND PRODUCTS.

The great extent of the country naturally implies an extremely varied climate. Cyrus the Great made this remark regarding the climate of his empire: "The people perish with cold at one extremity, while they are suffocated with heat at the other."

Persia may be considered to possess three climates: that of southern Dashtistan, one of the elevated plateau, and a third of the Caspian provinces. The spring and fall of the year are rainy seasons, but perfectly beautiful, while the summers are long, dry and hot, but not unpleasantly so excepting at midday. The atmosphere is clear and pure at all times.

The cultivated soil of Persia, wherever there is an abundance of rain or a possibility of irrigation, produces an immense variety of crops. The best wheat on the surface of the globe is grown here, other characteristic products being barley, rice, cotton, sugar cane, tobacco, millet, potatoes, sweet corn, cabbage, and all other garden vegetables found in other countries.

Great care has been taken to have brooks and streams, whether natural or artificial for the purpose of irrigating the land, lined on both sides with shade trees. This is most especially the case in Oroomiah Plain, so that this part of Persia has been named by travelers the Paradise of Persia. Wooded lands are found south of the Caspian Sea and one large forest in the vicinity of Shiraz. These forests are of very dense growth and contain oak, beech, elm, walnut, sycamore, ash, yew and juniper trees.

The mineral wealth of Persia is as yet undeveloped, excepting some modest efforts in coal, copper, iron and lead mining. The forests of the Elburz Mountains are infested with wild animals, such as wolves, tigers, jackals, wild boars, foxes, and the Caspian cat. Deer of every variety inhabit some of the mountains; lions and leopards are found in Mazandaron. Among the domestic animals are the horse, camel, buffalo, cow, ass, donkey, mule, sheep, dog, cat, etc. Persia is the home of the famous fat-tail sheep and produces also the much coveted lamb fur worn by ladies and called the Persian fur. Here also are found fine Arabian horses which may be termed the Oriental limited passenger trains or flyers, while the donkeys, mules and camels perform in the east the functions of western freight lines. Persian horses have always been celebrated as the finest in the east; they are larger and more handsome but not so fleet as those of Arabia. Sheep are one of the main sources of wealth in the country.

Among the flowers in Persia are the manigold, hollyhock, white lily, violet, tulip, chrysanthemum and roses of many kinds. The latter are cultivated in fields for the trade and the manufacture of "golab" or ottar of roses.

Poultry is good and plentiful. There are fowls, geese, ducks, turkeys, guineas, partridges, quails, doves, pheasants, as well as hawks, flamingos, crows, swans, storks, herrons, owls, cuckoos, hoo-poes and bul-buls or nightingales.

Cities like single dwellings are surrounded by high earthen walls about six feet thick and twenty feet in height. The gates within these walls are open during the day, but at 8 o'clock in the evening they are closed. No person can enter or leave the city after this hour and the people within the city walls might as well remain in doors, as the streets are shrouded in utter darkness, there being no system of street lighting whatever. Besides this no person is permitted to walk the streets after 9 o'clock p. m. When a nightwatch or guard (equal to our patrolman) happens to meet any one on the street after this hour, he will compel him to patrol the streets with him all night long, thumping and jerking him about and occasionally striking him in the neck or on the back unless he gives him some money. At 5:30 in the morning the wanderer is confined in a prison cell where he will have to remain until a ransom has been paid for him, the amount of which is determined by the chief of police. Persons whose duty or calling make it imperative to go out upon the streets after 9 p. m., such as physicians, nurses, etc., can do so unmolested provided they have been careful to get the password from the mayor of the city. Such a password is given out to the city officials by the mayor daily and any private person knowing it proves thereby that he or she has permission to be out after the respective hour.

The houses as a rule are built of sun dried bricks, but very few being made of burnt bricks. The homes of the poor contain but one large room. Some of these houses have rooms built upon the flat roof, which is reached by a flight of stairs built on the outside. Wealthy people live in well built two-story houses. In cities the houses are built closely adjoining, so that it is possible to walk all over the city on the house tops. This is the common way of traversing in winter when the streets are impassable owing to slush and mud. In some of the large cities such as Teheran, the capital, Ispahan and Shiraz, modern street paving is being introduced. Streets have no names, houses are not numbered, no police patrolmen during the day, no city directory is to be found. All information must be obtained from persons you chance to meet and find able and willing to give it, or else canvas from house to house until you reach your point. There are no newspapers of any kind and of course no advertising is done.

As you walk the streets you will hear the call to prayer when the Mollah, three times a day, stands on the roof of a minaret on a mosque and repeats the muezzin. But at times the throng crowding the narrow street is so dense as to prevent the Mollah from attending to his duty. Then a lord or government official may be seen with a company of from 50 to 200 soldiers, as the case may demand, going up and down the street to open the way for him to pass. Every person must stand still and bowing low push against a wall when an officer passes. A refusal to comply with this custom would put anyone in danger of being whipped to death.

Only one line of merchandise is sold on any one business street. On one you will find only dry goods; in another street nothing but groceries; a third contains iron, copper and silversmiths' shops, etc. The streets average thirty feet in width and many are arched over with brick arches, to shut out the rain and the snow. These covered streets are lighted by openings in the arches. Camels, horses, mules and donkeys, heavily laden with goods, may be seen passing through the streets, and in the open squares many of these animals may be seen that belong to strangers who have come to the city to buy or sell. At the entrances of some of the mosques one may see a Mollah or two, sitting down and acting as notary public, drawing up legal documents for men standing around and before him. For such a document they get from ten to fifteen cents.

In purchasing goods in Persia a foreigner is liable to be overcharged, as it is quite customary among dealers to advance the price on their goods to two or three times their real value, expecting to be obliged to lower the price before being able to make a sale. Silver and goldsmiths turn out some highly artistic work in the shape of rings, and belts for ladies. You cannot find a woman selling goods in a store or bazaar in all Persia, with the only exception of one single street in each city or village, where poor old women and widows are franchised to sell such articles as caps, purses, sacks, soaps, etc. Their faces, however, must be covered up entirely, with only two holes in the covering for the eyes. Only a few women from the lower classes are seen in the bazaars shopping, and they dare not have their faces exposed. No Christian is permitted to sell liquids such as milk, oil, syrups, or juicy fruit, like grapes, etc. Mohammedans are prohibited by law to buy things of this nature from a Christian, and, if on the other hand a Christian wishes to buy anything of this sort from a Mohammedan, he must not touch anything, as the merchant, should the Christian finally fail to take the goods, could never sell to a Mohammedan what has previously been touched or handled by a Christian.

THE BAZAAR AND CURRENCY.

The bazaars, which is a term including at the same time a salesroom, wareroom and manufactory, are in the center of the city. They are open after six in the morning and closed at six in the evening. Friday is the Mahommedan's sabbath day or day of rest, and all stores are closed. Whenever the bazaars are open passers by may see how goods are manufactured on a small scale. In the timber bazaar men saw boards with long hand-saws; a little further on carpenters manufacture doors, windows and coffins. So it is in the bazaars of the hatter, baker, blacksmith, confectioner and restaurant. Some are weaving cotton and silk cloths, carpets and shawls on hand-looms, though some of these goods are manufactured in villages and brought into the city for sale. Again, there are saddlers, turners, tailors, wood turners, etc.

The Persian standard of weights—

100 miskals	1 dirham.
4 dirhams	= 1 hef-ta.
8 hef-tas	= 1 batman.
4 batmans	= 1 khon-ka-rie.
10 batmans	= 1 load.
25 batmans	= 1 khalivar.

Copper and silver coins are in general use, while gold is scarce. Lately, paper money has been issued, both in Persian and English languages, but has met with but little favor. The Russian currency is also in circulation to some extent. The exchange is regulated by Europe and India. The numerous Persian bankers, called sarafs, have their abodes within the bazaars. Each saraf sits on a cushion in a small enclosure behind a little table covered with copper, silver and gold coins, for exchanging. These are of that kind whose tables our Lord Jesus overturned in the temple of Jerusalem. The mint at Teheran, established since 1878, was platted by Europeans but is now conducted by Persians.

Table of Persian currency, and its value—

5 denars	= 1 gaz-beh.	
30 denars	= 1 tem-bal.	
50 denars	= 1 shah-hi	= 6 tem-bal.
100 denars	= 1 yuz-al-tum	= 2 shah-hi.
500 denars	= 1 penabad	= 10 shah-hi.
1,000 denars	= 1 keran	= 20 shah-hi.

EDUCATION.

Every city or town has its schools for boys, located in the mosques and conducted by mollahs. There are no schools for girls, as it is not considered good policy to enlighten the female sex too much by giving them an education, and perchance making them dissatisfied with their present station in life. The attendance at school also for the boys is voluntary, no one being compelled to send his boys if he should prefer to keep them at home. Pupils pay the teacher all the way from five to twenty-five cents a month tuition; but such as are too poor to pay anything are admitted free of charge. The Mollah's sustenance is furnished him by the pupils daily in form of eatables of all kinds. These schools are attended by boys and youths ranging from ten to twenty years of age. Text-books for local history and poetry are in the Persian, the Koran and grammar are taught in the Arabic language; mathematics, geography, science and general history are never taught.

While preparing for their lessons, the pupils reel back and forth, repeat the words and sentences loud enough to be heard a long distance off. This they imagine to be an aid to memory. The teacher has authority to punish the pupil very severely. Parents will sometimes take a boy to school and deliver him over to the gentle keeping and care of the teacher with these words: "His bones are mine, but his flesh is yours. Teach him and punish him as you see fit."

A post is planted in the school-room. To this an unruly boy's feet are tightly fastened, soles upward, and the soles are then belabored with heavy switches. This is, however, applied only to the most unruly and wilfullest. For milder offenses, the teacher raps pupil over the head with a long switch, which is always kept in a convenient place or carried about with him by the teacher. Religious teachings are limited to quotations from the Koran and repeating the traditions about their prophets. The boys are generally very fond of reviling each other, and very quarrelsome. The teacher does not protect the weaker, but urges him on to return insinuations or blows. Frequently the pupils of one mosque attack those of another, regarding them as their enemies. The most prominent university of the Shute Mohammedans is in the shrine of Karballa.

All who wish to become Mushtaheds (see Priesthood) study at this place. In several large cities they have schools of higher rank than the ordinary mosque-school. In these the pupils are offered a course of Persian literature. We state with pleasure that the late Shah, after his visits to some of the European universities, has founded a college in his capital, which is called the abode of science. The French, English and Russian languages are taught here, and the study of some modern sciences are being introduced. This institute, however, is only available to princes and sons of wealthy people; it is only one pretty flower in the vast wilderness. The aim of Mohammedanism is to keep the masses ignorant, so that the priests may continue to rule over them. The entire priesthood, therefore, does not favor higher education. Some counts or lords send their sons to Paris, in France, to be educated, but the ordinary young man has no opportunities to acquire knowledge.

AGRICULTURE.

Persian people are largely employed in agriculture and grazing. Farmers go a long distance to work. Oxen, cows and buffaloes are used in plowing the fields. The plow is similar to the fork of a tree, the point being covered with iron or steel; the soil is scratched up and loosened somewhat to a shallow depth. Plowing is done three times in a season; then narrow ditches are drawn to divide the field and to irrigate it. The water from a river is turned into creeks to run the flouring mills, then divided into little brooks and streamlets and thus carried to the farms and fields. The seed is sown by hand, broadcast. Reapers or cradles are not used in harvesting, sickles or scythes taking their places. The blades of the agricultural implements are almost the same as those in the United States, but the handles are very small. A reaper cuts one handful of grain after another until a good sized bundle is cut; this he then binds into a sheaf, before cutting any more, and so forth. A person passing a field where a farmer is at work will greet him by saying, "May God give you strength," whereupon the farmer will reply, "You are welcome; may God keep you." But should the former be of the nobility, the farmer will pick up a sheaf of grain and lay before the visitor on the road. This is answered by the latter with a present of a few cents or whatever he may choose to give, according to his dignity.

When the time for threshing approaches the farmers have all the grain carried on horseback or by donkeys to the vicinity of the village where the threshing is to take place. Here the farmer takes sheaf after sheaf, unties it and throws it in a circle upon the bare ground, in the open air. Muzzled oxen are then led across it again and again, or round and round in the circle, to tramp the kernels out with their hoofs. In some places they employ a sort of machine, consisting of a roller about five feet long and one and a half feet high, with teeth or iron spikes spirally arranged on it. Above the roller is a seat for the driver, and when the machine is drawn the roller turns. When all the wheat is threshed it is left in a heap and the farmer waits for a strong wind; then with wooden grain forks the grain is thrown into the air and the wind blows the chaff away, while the kernels fall to the ground.

This is then carried to the mill, where it is ground into flour.

Numerous orchards yield all kinds of delicious fruit. Mulberry tree orchards are carefully raised and tended for feeding silk worms; apricots are cultivated in large orchards and the fruit dried both for the home market and for export; but a small part of the annual crop is kept for summer and winter use without cooking or canning it. Large vineyards employ thousands of people, and the grapes are probably among the best in the world and of endless variety, and the wine prepared from them is very palatable, not being at all adulterated. Large quantities of mollasses are also manufactured from grape juice, much of which is exported to Europe, via Austria. Two kinds of raisins are made from the grapes: the kishmish and the sabja. A plastered or cemented surface on the slope of a hill is covered with grapes, which are then converted into raisins by rays of the sun. These raisins are called kishmish. Water, turned into lye by the addition of ashes from a thornbush or burnt vines, is boiled and grapes dipped into it. After this they are spread out upon the ground to dry for a week. The very choicest raisins are made from seedless grapes. A strong, spiritous liquor, called arac, is manufactured from raisins by distillation.

A large part of the work connected with grazing consists in attending to the milch cows, sheep and goats. The milking of the latter affords quite a comical aspect. The gate or door of the goat pen is so low that the goat must lower her head to enter. While in the act of doing so the head is grasped and held firmly by one woman while another milks the goat. All milk is heated forthwith and most of it is turned into matsoon and cheese. The matsoon or yogurt is a curd gained by putting rennet into the boiled milk and letting it sour for several days. From the soured milk butter is made in churns. These are of several kinds. A large earthen jar, somewhat shaped like an egg, is filled with cream, the opening closed with a piece of leather and the jar laid down upon one side, whereupon it is rolled back and forward on the ground. Another churn is made from the hollowed trunk of a tree. It is suspended in the air by ropes and made to move similar to a swing. Cheese

is made by allowing the whey to flow off without
pressure. It is preserved by salt and sometimes mixed
with herbs for flavor, and buried.

Spinning and weaving dress goods, carpets and other
fabrics are universal household occupations. Wool is
carded by pulling it over a pair of long-toothed brass
combs. Wool and silk are sometimes spun on a distaff,
whirled by hand, but more frequently a spin-wheel is
used, the spinner sitting upon the floor and managing
the thread partly with her feet. In many villages are
little shops where silk is spun on a small machine. The
cocoons are thrown into a caldron of boiling water
mixed with milk. A man turns a wheel, about a yard
in diameter, by means of a petal, and with one hand
stirs the cocoons to loosen the fibre, while with the
other hand he draws up the thread to be wound around
the wheel. The refuse and stray fibres are spun by the
women and made into head-dresses. In the orchards of
mulberry trees, where the leaves are gathered for feeding the worms, the trees are kept trimmed so that each
occupies but one square yard of ground. The seed
worms complete their work in three months and are
kept in the house during the winter months. The
annual silk crop of Persia, produced chiefly in the Caucasian provinces, amounts to 600,000 pounds.

Furniture is not in use in Persia, as people eat, sit
and sleep on the floor, which is made of hard wood and
covered with mattings and rugs or carpets. Bedding is
spread out upon the floor for the night, rolled up and
stowed away for the day. No knives and forks are used
while eating. Traveling is done mostly on the back of
animals and is very unsafe, the roads being infested
with Kurds, robbers and highwaymen. This accounts
for the custom of traveling in large companies called
caravans. Passengers find no accommodations excepting
at the caravansories, and even there nothing is fur-

nished, but they must carry everything with them, even
to a cup from which to drink, or a chair or rug upon
which to sit. The only railway in Persia is a short
line, twenty-four miles long, from the Shah's residence
to his summer resort. The public roads and highways
are in a deplorable condition, and very few carriage
roads to be found. All merchandise is conveyed upon
the backs of animals, these forming long lines in their
journey across the dreary plains.

Women are ignorant and superstitious, morality
among them very low. But few can read, and almost
all continuously smoke a kalion or water pipe. They
are generally married at the age of 12 years and are
regarded as very much inferior by their husbands. (See
Social and Domestic Life in Persia.)

Many manners and customs which we find mentioned
in the Bible are still in vogue in this country at this
present day; they still place the blind and crippled along
the wayside to ask for alms; they yet pray on the house-
tops, and the salutations, traffic, building, travel and
farming have undergone no radical changes in the last
2,000 years.

The Nobleman.

The nobility of Persia lead a life of luxury. Such
titles as counts and lords are not obtained by conspicuous service to the nation or country, nor by proficiency
in knowledge and learning, but by descendancy, and
many an ignorant and unworthy person bears them.
Wealthy merchants also purchase them for their off-
spring. The titled class in Persia is very numerous.
In a city of 60,000 inhabitants there are more than 500
counts. They own the bulk of the Persian soil. In
some instances one count owns as many as one hundred villages. The poor rayat or tenant must pay his
landlord one-half or two-thirds of all the produce of his

farm. Aside from this a poll tax and a tax on his house must be paid. His cattle, sheep and goats are taxed, he must deliver unto his landlord two fowls, two loads of fuel, and a quantity of eggs annually, and when his sons or daughters are married a marriage fee must be paid. His meadows and orchards are also taxed, and only the yoke of oxen with which he tills the ground are excepted from taxation. But this is not all. He is literally at the mercy of his agha or master, a name which very correctly expresses the relation between landlord and peasant. The landlord legally may demand three days of labor from his rayat without paying for it, but in reality he makes them work for him as much as he pleases. Whenever he pays a visit at one of his peasant's houses, he simply and unceremoniously appropriates whatever he condescends to find worthy of taking. The peasant is held to buy his grain and flour from his landlord and must silently pay for these things whatever price the master puts on them, even far above the market price. For the slightest offense he is subjected to severe chastisement, being even ordered by his master to be tied and cruelly beaten.

And to all this and even more and worse outrages must the poor peasant submit, for fear of still greater persecutions in case of complaint. Christians have more to bear than Moslem neighbors; they are inferior beings—"infidels," "Christian dogs." The meanest Mohammedan is considered better than they. A Christian may not eat with a Moslem; he must not enter their houses with moist clothing. If struck by a Mohammedan he dares not strike back. In the courts he is not considered their equal; his life and property are not equally secure. Should a Mohammedan, for example, take a fancy to the daughter of a Christian, even at the tender age of 7 or 10 years, he will take her to his harem. An appeal to the governor would avail nothing, as it would simply be answered by the statement that she has declared to turn Mohammedan. She is lost to her family and religion forever, and should the parents ever so much argue that the child is too young to decide upon her own religion, or that she in all probability has been cajoled or frightened into making the change, or should the parents plead ever so much to be allowed an interview with her for just a few moments—she remains where she has been taken and grows up an inmate of a harem!

By Persian law all converts to the Islam may claim a lion's share of their father's estate. It therefore pays indigent Mohammedans well to entice young daughters of well-to-do Christians away from their homes.

Here is another instance: The governor demanded from a merchant an amount far in excess of the just taxes. The merchant refused. The result was that the governor took away all his property. To seek redress, the merchant petitioned the Shah and graciously received a royal order to the governor to have his possessions restored to him. Full of cheer and good hope the merchant traveled back and presented the written order to the governor. After reading the decree the governor looked keenly at the man for a moment, and then exclaimed, derisively: "Ha! You thought you could frighten me by reporting me to the Shah! You are indeed a brave man. Little did I expect you to be a man of so much courage. But so brave a man must needs have a brave heart. This brave heart of yours I must see, so as to learn courage from it." Then in a subdued tone he gave the order to his servants: "Take out that man's heart!" The servants immediately fell upon the merchant, slew him on the spot, tore out his heart and presented it to the governor on a tray.

The most common and most painful form of torture now in use is Persia is the bastinado.

BASTINADO.

The mechanical part of a bastinado is a pole, called a "Pellek," about eight feet in length, with a transverse handle at either end and loops of rope or leather in the middle. The man to be bastinadoed is laid back downward on the ground and, after his shoes and stockings are removed, his feet are passed through the loops. The pole is held by two soldiers at nearly the length of the man's legs from the ground, and by them it is turned until his ankles are so tightly secured that he cannot writhe out of them. In turning the pole the soles of the feet are brought upward, making them a fair mark for the flogger. Close by will be a large number (usually hundreds) of sticks with which the victim's feet are to be beaten. They are ordinary willow wands five or six feet long. The bark is left on, and the willows are kept wet to prevent them from breaking easily. Two or more expert floggers, clad in scarlet coats, bound in black, the uniform of the Shah's executioners, take their places near the pole, each armed with a stick with which they in turn

BELABOR THE VICTIM'S SOLES

until the stick is broken. Before the thrashing is commenced the victim is adjured to confess. If he does not the torture is kept up until he does, or until the supply of sticks gives out. Often 200 and 300 sticks are worn out before a confession is secured, although the torture often results in death, if the victim is aged or sick. All Persians are liable to this punishment, from the prime minister downward. The minister of finances was on one occasion given 400 lashes.

The bastinado is by no means the only mode of torture used in Persia to make criminals confess. Needles are run under the finger-nails of some prisoners until a confession is extorted, and it is a practice to cut

—95

gashes in the soles of a prisoner's feet, inserting therein broken glass, so that it is impossible for him to run away. Such punishments have been in vogue for ages, notwithstanding the fact that the late Shah years ago issued a firman prohibiting the torture of criminals.

DISFIGURING EVIL-DOERS.

For ordinary crimes in Persia, the punishment is personal disfigurement. The evil-doer who is caught in his evil-doing is marked for life. For a first offense at highway robbery, the prisoner may lose some of his fingers. For a second offense he is likely to lose a hand. The traveler passing through Persia for the first time is astonished at the number of maimed and half-blind men whom he meets on the caravan trails. The writer has seen one man in Persia who, as a result of persistent wrong-doing, had lost a hand, a foot, an ear and an eye. With all that he was pointed out as a person to be avoided.

Apart from the affliction of pain as a means of extorting confessions, there is another well defined reason for the torture of criminals. It is intended that corporal punishment shall be a warning and an example to other evil-doers. It is for this reason that the severed hands, fingers and ears of convicted men are thrown into one of the principal streets to horrify men going about the ordinary affairs of business.

HOW THE HEADS ARE CUT OFF.

Decapitation in Persia has lost some of its old-time picturesqueness. In thinking of a decapitation, one naturally pictures a scene in which the executioner, posed in a theatrical attitude, swings aloft a glittering scimetar, and with "one well-directed blow" strikes off the victim's head. In Persia today one finds that sort of thing only in picture-books imported from the

SAMNITES FEASTING

PERSIAN LORD AND ATTENDANTS.

Christian west. As a matter of prosaic fact, the victim's head is hacked off with a short knife. To be even more exact, the head is very rarely actually hacked off. Usually the executioner is satisfied with hacking open two or three large veins of the throat, and letting his man bleed to death. The traveler loses a great many illusions in a journey through Persia, and this is one of them.

Counts and lords are the most immoral class of people in all Persia. They are illiterate, know nothing of geography, mathematics or political economy, though most of them can read and write their own language and have a limited knowledge of local history. It is not at all surprising that such indolent, voluptuous people grow immoral, for among them it is considered a disgrace to do work of any kind.

Teheran, the capital of Persia, is called the "City of the Shadow of God," the "Footstool of the King of Kings." It has no glorious past to boast of. Though the neighboring plains contain mounds and ruins of great cities, it was only in the latter part of the past century that Teheran emerged from obscurity. The first records describe it as a village of underground hovels, affording a retreat from the summer heat or from the ravages of plundering hordes. She was chosen as the capital of Aga Mohammed Khan, the founder of the present Kajar dynasty. His preference for it was undoubtedly owing to its proximity to his own tribe in Mezandaran. Now, Teheran has assumed the position of the political center of central Asia. Here the legations of England, France, Russia, Germany, Austria, Holland, Turkey and the United States represent their respective countries and spin the webs of their political intrigues.

In a century Teheran's population has increased from 15,000 to 200,000 inhabitants. Owing to its modern growth, it has also partaken of a European element more than any other Persian city, and is more influenced by western ideas. The old style is yet noticeable in the high walls and deep moat surrounding the entire city. On each side of it are two large, well built and handsomely ornamented gates. On the other hand, broad avenues, well paved and bordered by shade trees, houses of modern architecture, embassy grounds, laid out after the pattern of an English park, phaetons and carriages, telegraph poles, tramways, gas and electric lights in the streets, drug stores, photograph galleries, strongly attest that western life has invigorated the stereotyped east. The bazaars also, while presenting the same general characteristics as in other cities, have wider aisles, and enjoy more of the much-needed sunlight. They are well stocked with imports, and those which deal in European goods attract the briskest trade.

The royal palace is surrounded by high stone walls. Four beautiful gates afford entrance to the grounds. On the sides of and above the gates the walls are adorned with the pictures of former kings and brave generals, and skillfully carved with lions' heads, the standards of Persia, and birds. The park-like grounds are beautifully arranged and kept; all the drives and walks lead to the Shah's palace, situated in the center, and are gorgeously ornamented with decorative trees and hedges of roses of varied hues. Numerous officers of superior rank guard the entrances and the walks and avenues that lead to the palace, those nearest to it ever standing with drawn sword. While hearing a case or passing judgment the king sits on his "peacock throne" surrounded by his cabinet, consisting of six advisers. His decisions, however, are absolute and may at any time overrule the opinion of his cabinet. This body forms the legislature of the country. The members of it appointed by the Shah, the people having no voice whatever in governmental affairs. Whenever the Shah feels tired his secretary reads to him from the "Sana-meh," a poetical history of Persian kings. It is one of the Shah's duties to make himself thoroughly acquainted with Persian history and the history of her former rulers. On retiring at night the entrance to the Shah's private room is guarded by two trustworthy officers with unsheathed swords. One of the four gates in the wall around the palace is called the Shah's gate, as he always enters through it. No other person, be he lord, count or high official, is permitted to pass through this gate on horseback or in a vehicle. He must dismount and walk through.

When the Shah goes from the palace for a chase or on a vacation, he is escorted by a large retinue, headed by about thirty footmen, each bearing a golden staff and shouting: "Disperse, disperse!" Hereupon the passage is immediately cleared so that the royal cavalcade may pass unmolested. The footmen are followed by about fifty men on horseback with drawn swords; next come ten or twelve riderless Arabian steeds dancing along, beauties of their race, adorned with bridles of gold studded with precious stones.

The Shah of Persia is in possession of the greatest and most valuable collection of jewels on the globe. These may be inspected in his palace, where they are heaped up in glass cases like tea or rice. His "peacock throne," which was brought from Delhi, India, by King Nadirsha, who captured that city about 200 years ago, has been estimated at $12,500,000 some years ago, and has risen in value since then. It is made of solid gold inlaid with diamonds, pearls and other jewels. The rug upon which the Shah prays is valued at $2,500,000. He has a tobacco pipe worth $500,000. His table is furnished with all the luxuries and good things in the land. There will be perhaps fifty or more different dishes served at one meal. When the Shah sits down to partake of some food he will glance over all these, but only touch or nibble from one or the other food, yet all the different courses must be prepared. From the time of the purchase until it appears upon the table, all food and drink is examined by two trustworthy inspectors, whose duty it is to see that the ruler is not poisoned. Again the food is inspected by the Shah's physician before eating a meal.

Persian law is divided into two departments—the Shahr and the Urf. The former is administered by the Mollahs, or priests, and is based upon the Koran. The latter is the oral law administered by secular judges, who decide cases to equity and traditions, or precedents orally handed down.

As the Urf is administered independently of the Shahr, an increase of powers would gradually result in the extinction of the latter. It is undoubtedly the aim of the government to bring about such a change, as one of the most important factors in promoting the elevation of Persia to the plane of modern progress, but any effort in this direction can be pursued only with great shrewdness and caution, for the Mollahs are naturally violently opposed to any abridgement of their power. In a general way the Urf takes cognizance of criminal cases and the Shahr of civil ones. The criminal is tried before the hakem or ket-hodah of a town or village; in the awarding of penalties, however, he follows the rules prescribed by the Shahr so far as they have not passed into desuetude.

Sometimes a criminal case is appealed directly to the governor of the province or to the Shah himself. This is especially the case if one of the parties involved is in any way connected with the government. The Shah or the governor concerns himself little with the law in such events, but decide at once, and with a word, a gesture, decrees retribution or reward. But although all questions not of a civil nature are by custom relegated to the decisions of the Urf, it is not uncommon for the judge to allow a case to be appealed to the Shahr when it is of special difficulty, or when the rank of the party is such as to make him dread the consequences of his decision. Any decision rendered by the religious expounders of the Shahr is accepted without demur as final; the sacredness of the Shahr and the sanctity of those who administer decisions based upon it make it impossible to dispute the decisions of that august tribunal. While, therefore, the Urf occupies a prominent place in the administration of justice, the Shahr continues by far the most important legal authority of the land, and it is by a study of that code and the methods of administering it that one can alone form any correct conception of the administration of justice in Persia.

The Shahr consists of a vast collection of dicta applying to every conceivable situation in life. Like the theocratic codes of other Mussulmans it is based on the Koran, but differs from them in the fact that it is enlarged and fortified by the opinions of the twelve Holy Imams, these Imams being considered by the Sheahs to be the true caliphs and their opinions having scarcely less weight than if delivered from the Almighty.

Early in the rise of Mohammedism it was the custom of the disciples of the Prophet to have recourse to him for explanation or expansion of the vague declarations of the Koran. After his death these commentaries were generally transmitted orally, and were called traditions, becoming in time very voluminous, so that it was necessary to reduce and codify them, adding opinions regarding the more obscure enactments. Hence the authority of the Holy Imams. The code of Persia treats of religious rites and duties; of contracts and obligations; of matters relating to the person; and of laws relating to cheese, meats and drinks, legal procedure, and the specification of penalties both from a religious and a civil point of view. Many of the laws of the Shahr are based on sound reason, and in their application are not unlike the laws of other countries.

Some of the features of the Shahr are as follows: Any man is forbidden to say his prayers in the presence of any women who, either at his side or before him, are also praying, whether praying together with him or alone; and without regard to the character of the woman, whether she be wife or within the forbidden degree of kinship, or a stranger. If the woman is behind the man at such a distance that in prostrating herself she cannot touch his feet, then the man also may do his praying.

One should avoid praying before an open fire, before the painted or graven figures or images of animate objects, or the stable of horses, asses or mules; but it is permitted in a sheepfold. One is forbidden to pray in an apartment wherein there is a fire-worshiper; the presence of a Christian or a Jew is unimportant. One should avoid having an open book before him, and should not pray before an overhanging wall or in a room where there is a pot de chambre.

"He who is dumb must wag his tongue while mentally repeating his prayers. The spot where the forehead should touch (during the genuflections of prayer) should be on the same horizontal plane on which the feet rest; nevertheless, one may exceed this line by the thickness of one brick or more."

Such are a few examples of the 549 laws respecting religious worship. The regulations concerning fasting and pilgrimage number no less than 1,012.

The law of sales includes 625.

"It is permissable to sell a piece of cloth or of land simply by a general exhibition of them to the purchaser, without obliging him to make a minute inspection."

Proof by taste or smell is indispensable when the object of sale is eatable or smellable. Articles of such a nature that they cannot be tested without breaking them such as nuts, melons or eggs, may be sold in ignorance of the condition of the contents; and in the event of the purchaser finding them defective, he has the right to interest and damages, but not to a return of the article.

"It is not permitted to sell fruits on the tree before they are shaped, that is, before the kernel is formed, but when they have reached that state they may be sold.

"After it is matured, fruit may be sold with or without the tree. It is not permitted to sell the fruits green in color (at maturity) before they become green.

It is recommended to the purchaser of a slave to change his name; to cause him to eat sweetmeats at the time, and to offer alms. One should avoid counting or weighing the purchase money for a slave in his presence. Slaves are thought a great deal of in Persia. As a rule masters are very kind to them, so that not seldom one may hear a master addressed by his slave with "My father," and the master in replying will call him "My son." Slaves are well taken care of in clothing and nourishment. They differ in color and value. The "Habshi" are the most expensive; the "Somali" range next in price; the Negro slave being the cheapest in price, and only employed as cooks. One good "Habshi" will bring $250; a good "Somali," $150, while the market price for the best among the Negro slaves, which are taxed according to their strength, is but $70.

Not less than 1,412 different chapters are used in the Shahr for subjects on marriage and divorce, besides a large number on concubinage, slaves and rearing of children.

The prophet hath said, "Marry and establish a family;" the most wicked among the dead are the celibates; he who desires to contract a marriage should seek after a woman combining four requisites: legitimate birth, virginity, prolificness and chastity. One should not be content with beauty and riches; it is even forbidden to marry with these points alone in view. Marriage should not be consumated while the moon is in the sign of the scorpion; during an eclipse of the moon; on a day when there will be an eclipse of the sun; at noon; towards the end of twilight; during the last three days of the month*; between dawn and sunrise; during the first night of each month, excepting the month of Ramazan; during the middle night of the month; while on a journey; in a tempest, nor during an earth-quake.

When marriage is being proposed to a maiden, her silence is equivalent to a consent. The consent of a widow, however, or a divorce, must be audibly pronounced to be legally valid. Any man may form as many temporary marriages as he chooses. If the husband desires one of his wives to accompany him on a journey, the selection is made by casting the lot. Husbands are recommended to treat all their wives alike.

Divorce is pronounced by a husband in the presence of not less than two witnesses. In doing this, one of three statutory formulas must be used, any other version, though expressing the intention ever so clearly, are invalid. He must either say "Ente talekun," (thou art divorced) or "Felanet talekun" (such a one is divorced), or "Hazee talekun" (this person is divorced). The Arabic formula must always be used.

---

*The last three days of a month are called el mohak, which signifies the moon is below the horizon.

There are also three kinds of divorce, one by virtue of which the husband cannot take back the divorced wife; one with this privilege reserved; and the temporary divorce, for the purpose of proving whether the woman is pregnant by a husband from whom she was previously divorced. The irrevocable divorce is brought about when a husband pronounces the formula of divorce upon a wife whom he has twice before taken as his wife again. The temporary marriage is an institution peculiar to Persia and abhored by all Mohammedans elsewhere. The Shahrs defend it on the plea that it was not prohibited by the Prophet, and consequently must be right, according to a fundemental principle of their law that whatsoever is not prohibited by law is allowed. The most important feature of the temporary matrimony, however, is the dowry paid by the husband; without this parents would scarcely permit their daughters to enter into it. Four conditions are indispensable to the legality of such a marriage—the contract, the personal conditions, the dowry, and the stipulated time for which the marriage is contracted. The contract is legal and binding only when it has been drawn in legal form before or by a Mollah. As to the duration of such a temporary marriage the law provides no limit, the matter being settled by mutual agreement; may it be for a fraction of a day or for ninety-nine years; it may even antedate the day when the contract is written if so desired by both parties.

Penalties for fornication, adultery, sodomy and similar vices are very severe, lapidation being the most common upon repetition of the last named, and for the conviction of the first named even after the first offense. Not less than 395 chapters treat of the laws of procedure. To administer the Shahr a judge must be of legal age, sound of mind, faithful in performing the duties of the Islam, of reputable life, of legitimate birth, well instructed and of the male sex. He should also be endowed with a good memory, for one who lacks this faculty is incapable of properly exercising judicial functions.

The principle which regulates the Mussulman's connubial life he expresses when upon any occasion, but most often before his marriage he will say to his wife: "It is my *privilege* to love many women, and it is your *duty* to love *only* me. Now attend thou to thy duty and I will see to my privilege." Taking a walk with his wife a Mohammedan would be disgraced should she go before him or by his side; she must obediently follow behind. For wife murder a man can be fined a sum of money, but the law will not find him guilty of homicide, as woman is not considered equal to man before the law. A man meeting a woman anywhere in public or private will not salute her, but the woman is expected to greet him with a courteous nod.

Priesthood.

Men who expound and administer the Shahr are either Mushtaheds or Mollahs. The chief Mushtahed must have taken a course with the great Mushtahed of Kerbellah, near Bagdad, who dwells ever at the tomb of Ali. The highest Mushtahed in Persia, the chief justice of the supreme court, as it were, is at present Hagdi Mollah Ali. When he goes abroad he is mounted on a white mule and followed by one single attendant, but the multitude disperses before him as if he were a supernatural being. A word from him would hurl the Shah from his throne, or doom all Christians and foreigners in the county. In his presence even the Shah stands.

The Mushtahids are graded into four degrees, the fourth being the lowest grade and numerically the strongest. Their means of existence consists in drawing up legal documents, performing marriage ceremonies and accepting presents. For the marriage of a couple they charge a large fee. Common people consider it a great privilege to give a present to a Mushtahid, and a favor on his part if he accepts it. These men, in consequence, are generally very rich and own one or more beautiful palaces. Rich ladies feel highly honored to be chosen as the wife of a Mushtahid.

A Mollah's duty is to visit the sick, call on families and teach them prayers and make them familiar with the traditions, and conduct funeral ceremonies. Some also teach the boys, who go to them daily for instruction. Their meals are furnished by the pupils, each bringing something to eat for the Mollah (usually choice morsels) every morning. Besides this each pupil pays one dime tuition a month. In autumn the Mollah is provided for the winter by his parishioners, who bring him a collection of grapes, apples, wheat, fuel, etc. He is highly respected among the community and is always invited by some family on holidays. He also draws up legal documents and letters for the people and receives as a remuneration from two to ten cents; but he is quite often paid in the form of two or three eggs, a basket of fruit, and the like. This is the poor Mollah's only income. Some have charge and do secular work for a living, others recite Koran on the sepulchre of a lord, for which they are rewarded by the relatives of the deceased. I have seen a Mollah who recited Koran for fifteen years at the tomb of a noted army officer.

There is yet another class of priests, more learned and more devout than the rest, who act as revivalists. On holidays, which occur quite frequently, the mosques are usually crowded with worshipers. Then one of these priests will mount an elevated pulpit very ostensibly, and in an impressive tone begin to read or repeat Koran. He will chant traditions on the lives and deeds of the prophets and martyrs and relate pathetic stories of the noble sacrifice of departed heroes of faith. His charming tones and imploring utterances have much effect on his audience and men and women weep and strike against their bosoms.

Persia acknowledges Ali as the Caliph after Mohammed. The descendants of Ali are therefore held in high esteem and rank among the noblest families in Persia. They are called Say-yids (prophets or masters) and enjoy privileges denied other men. They are very zealous in perpetuating their own caste. From Ali's time they have kept a careful record of their genealogy. This family record, called Sajjara, is handed down from father to son and serves as a credential to the Say-yid tribe. Each family must possess a credential of this kind, at least 200 years old. Should it be worn by age and use, the heads of families may draft copies and duly certify to them. The Say-yid may be easily distinguished by his garments. He wears a green turban and girdle. Should a common man assume to wear such he would be severely punished. The Say-yid's turban is to him more precious than a king's crown; it is the emblem of his glory—the girdle a symbol of strength. Their rank is higher than any other in the country, and their high-priest is more honored than a prince. So the Say-yid rules over other men. He demands and receives their homage. In the assemblies of lords and influential men the Say-yid occupies a foremost seat and is always served first. Solemn oaths are delivered by their heads; all men fear them, believing that their curse will surely come to pass. They are never smitten or reviled.

If ever a Christian should raise his hand against a Say-yid, that hand must certainly be severed from his body. Say-yids are exempt from all legal punishment. Governors cannot impose fines or imprisonment on them. Should a Say-yid kill a common person, it would be impossible to have him in turn suffer a death penalty, for this would be a sin against God for it is universally believed that God created all other men for the sake of Mohammed and his descendants; hence a Sayyid's punishment must come through the leader of that order. Many promises and vows are made to them. Parents having a sick daughter will vow to marry her to a Say-yid, should she recover, believing that God will take the disease away in the Say-yids behalf.'

The Say-yids generally ride gray horses, and claim that all horses of that particular color belong to them. They conduct the large caravans, which start out annually to worship the tomb of Ali. Their presence is supposed to protect the caravans from thieves and robbers. By virtue of their law, one tenth of all property is addicted to them. The majority of them do not work, but live well on the merits of their position as Say-yids, or holy men. The more noble among them will sit in their houses and receive tithes of fruit, coffee, tea and money, of the surrounding people. When these are not willingly given, a servant will be sent with authority to demand and take them. The less noble Say-yid will go in person to the houses, vineyards and gardens, and gather his portion.

The Order of the Dervishes

is one of the holiest orders among the Moslems. They are men who have voluntarily consecrated their lives to Allah and his Prophet. Parents in many cases dedicate their sons to the order. Quite often, childless women will vow to Allah to consecrate a son he will graciously give, back to him, by having him enter into the order of Dervishes. This order numbers members from all classes of society, high and low, wealthy and indigent, even from the royal family.

A Dervish is expected to be and commonly is humble, kind and liberal, ready to do anyone a service. He suffers all sorts of hardships, self imposed, and leads a very humble life, for this to him is holiness. He is required to be well informed in all religious stories, traditions, and the Koran, and particularly in the poetical writings of the Maw-le-wi order, (which is their own order), founded by Au-wa-ri, the father of the Dervises. Some of the members know from one to five thousand of these sacred poems. The majority are sufficiently well educated to read, and in general they are the most faithful, honest and pure followers of Mohammed. Some are very intelligent and well educated and perfectly familiar with all their religious rites and rituals. On the other hand they are exceedingly superstitious, fanatical and ambitious to propogate their religion, believing it to be a true religion. Their main occupation is to sit in the streets during the week days and tell stories, tales and traditions. Their poems glorify Mohammed and Ali, God's supremest creatures. One of these poems runs in this strain: "The first of creatures is Ali; the supreme of beings is Ali; the true Caliph of the Prophet is Ali; the Lord of all the world is Ali; the Lord of my soul is Ali."

The Dervishes wear long hair and a pointed, orange-shaped cap, a cloak of patch work and a long white robe. In their right hand they carry a tomahawk or hatchet with a fancy handle; on the blade are some inscriptions consisting of passages from the Koran, or poems. In the left hand they hold a kashkul or receptacle for money donated them. A dozen or more may be seen on every street not far distant from each other, standing in front of the stores singing some poems for the praise of Ali in a loud voice, and with an earnest and enthusiastic spirit. Then he will pass his kashkul and the shopkeeper will drop into it some small coin or only a bit of sugar or ginger. Any gift is acceptable. Sometimes they are called Kalander, which means humble and holy men of Allah. They are exempted from tax and from military service. Many presents are given to them by the people. The salutation is different from that among common people. The first says, "Ya-ho" (O living God); the response is, "Ya-mal-ho" (O God, the Giver of life;" "Ya hak, Ya hak" (O truth, O truth).

Among Mush-ta-hids, two tithes are given to those who excel in holiness, viz: Pish-Namiz and Imam-Juma. The former means mediator in prayer; the latter, the prophet of holy Friday.

They are indeed more devoted to their faith, and at the same time more fanatical in their hatred against Christianity. When one of these priests goes to the mosque, he wears a large turban on his head, a cloak of fur, a staff with gold or silver handle. He wears a long beard, which is painted black. Following him is a procession of from fifty to one hundred men, mostly mollahs, or lower class who are faithful Moslems. Proceeding toward the mosque with slow and solemn tread, he is saluted by people of all classes along the street by their rising to their feet, crossing the breast with the arms and reverently bowing before him, uttering the words, "Sallam ali-Kun Agha" (peace be unto you, sir). This service occurs on holy Friday.

Women are not admitted in these most holy and solemn services. The Mush-ta-hid stands in the front part of the mosque, facing Mecca, and all the audience is back of him. As he advances in the prayer, all the people repeat what he prays. They imitate every motion he makes. When he kneels, they kneel. When he puts the ends of his front fingers in his ears, the entire audience does the same. They believe all prayers prayed in that way are accepted through his mediatorial prayer.

The people are called to the mosque to pray at daylight, noon and dusk, by a priest who stands on the roof of the mosque. Calling them the priest will go to the pulpit and take out of his pocket a piece of clay or wood from Mahomet's burying ground, and laying it down on the ground will kiss it, turning towards the four cardinal points. While doing this, the congregation will do this fifteen times, kissing the ground, then they will go to the service of reading and prayer.

Reading is largely from the Koran and other religious books.

The Moslem always washes with cold water before prayer. He will take a jar of water and say: "Bism Allah" (In the name of God I do this holy service). Then, dipping his right hand in the water, he rubs his arms from the wrist to the elbow, with the tips of his fingers he will wet his forehead and the inside of his ears, and the surface of his feet. Travelers in the desert use sand as a substitute for water.

The worshiper must have a seal, a piece of clay or wood from Mohammed's burying ground, the size of a dollar; on it are written the words, "There is no God but God." Facing Mecca, he puts the seal on the ground and standing erect he raises both hands to his head, kneels to the ground, puts his brow on the seal, then kisses it. Rising to his feet he puts both index fingers in his ears, and makes numerous other gestures.

The common place of prayer is the mosque, but few of the Moslems pray there, as they prefer praying in the streets, open squares and in meadows before mosques where they will be seen by more men and can better show their piety and integrity. In the midst of his prayer he will stop and speak a few words to the surrounding

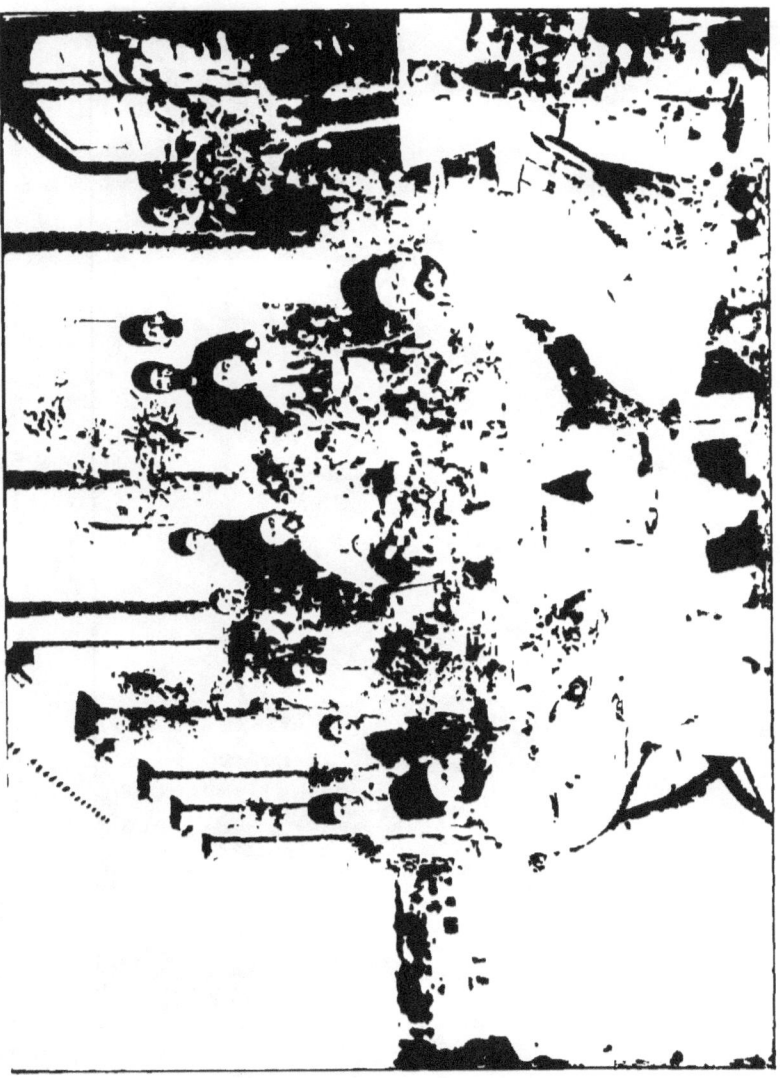

LORD AT OROOMIAH, PERSIA, WITH HIS FRIENDS.

BASTINADO.

people as a religious custom, or to revile children whose noise while at play may have interrupted him.

The official prayer of Islam, which is used throughout all the Mohammedan countries and is daily repeated in the Cairo University by ten thousand Mohammedan students from all countries, reads thus:

"I seek refuge with Allah, from Satan the accursed, in the name of Allah, the compassionate, the merciful. O Lord of all creatures, O Allah, destroy the infidels and thine enemies, the enemies of religion. O Allah, make their children orphans and defile their abodes. Cause their feet to slip. Give them and their families, their children, household and woman and relations by marriage, their brothers and friends, their possessions and their race, their wealth and lands as booty to the Mussulman, O Lord of all creatures!"

Here are some of the commandments of the Koran:

(1) They are surely infidels who say: "Verily God is Christ, the son of Mary." Koran, chapter 5.

(2) O true believers, take not the Jews or Christians for your friends; they are friends to each other; but whosoever among you taketh them for friends, he is surely one of them. Koran, chapter 5.

(3) War is enjoined upon you against the infidels, but this is hateful unto you; yet perchance ye hate a thing which is better for you, and perchance ye love a thing which is worse for you; but God knoweth and ye know not. Koran, chapter 2.

(4) Fight therefore against them until there be no temptation to idolatry, and the religion be God's. Koran, chapter 2.

(5) Fight against the friends of Satan for the stratagem of Satan is weak. Koran, chapter 4.

(6) And when the months wherein ye are not allowed to attack them shall be past, kill the idolators wheresoever ye shall find them, and take them prisoners and

besiege them and lie in ambush for them in every convenient place. Koran, chapter 9.

(7) When ye encounter the unbelievers strike off their heads until ye have made a great slaughter among them. Koran, chapter 47.

(8) Ye are also forbidden to take to wife free women who are married except those women whom your right hand shall possess as slaves. This is ordained you from God."

So you see they have for a guide in this life the Koran and the reward hereafter, Paradise.

The Moslems have only one month of fasting called the ramazan. Their month begins with the new moon, but sometimes in some parts of the land it is cloudy and they cannot see the moon. So men will be appointed by the government throughout all the empire to watch carefully for the new moon, sometimes from the peaks of mountains. They will fast from one hour before sunrise to one-half hour after sunset, or till it becomes too dark for a man to discriminate between red and black thread. During this time they abstain from eating, drinking and smoking. The poor class work till noon. The rich do not work at all. The most of the day is spent in reciting the Koran, praying in the street, for the Moslems might long to eat also, or even take a taste and thus break their fast.

Boys and girls above 7 years must fast, while sick men are not compelled to during this month. However, when they recover they are required to fast thirty days as soon as they are able. They do not converse much in the day, but wear a sad countenance. They do not allow a Christian to speak to them. At morning and evening in the cities a cannon is fired for the beginning and ending of the fast. During this month much alms is given. The lords and princes especially send meals from their table. They believe fasting and alms giving will secure absolute forgiveness of sins and admittance to heaven. The night is changed to a feast. They eat and drink and converse till twelve o'clock. Then they retire, but are up again at three and eat and drink till one hour before sunrise.

Death among them occurs most often in that month because many eat too much. So many different meals hurt their stomach and they fall sick and die.

While this fasting is easy for the rich, as they can sleep all day and keep awake all night, it is a heavy burden to the poor, who must work during the day, especially when the fasting comes in the farming season. The month, however, in course of time has been changed. They are also strictly prohibited from doing much talking in this month of fasting that they may not obtain much air.

Many observe the fast faithfully, but often through fear of persecution.

The pilgrimage is strictly commanded to Mohammedans. There are many places to be visited, but the most important is Medina, the burial place of Mohammed. The second place is Mecca, Mohammed's birthplace. This city is the most holy to all the Mohammedan world. Here is the old temple of the Arabs, the Kaaba, which was converted by Mohammed into a mosque. The third place is Karballa. It is situated near Bagdad, where the most leaders of the religion live. The fourth place is Mashhad. This city is situated in the northeast part of Persia, in the state of Khorasan, near the Caspian Sea. This is the most holy city in Persia. Here many famous persons lie buried, as, for instance, the grandchildren of Mohammed.

This mosque is richer than Mecca and Karballa. The dome is lined with gold outside and inside. Generally each king of Persia makes expensive presents, but the most remarkable event in this connection was

200 years ago. Nadirshah, a powerful king of Persia, who conquered India and despoiled Calcutta of its treasures, made a present to this temple of a crown of gold, adorned with precious stones.

Mohammedan law commands all to go to these holy places. Books of ceremony emphasize the importance of such pilgrimage. The hope of remission of sins is given to all visitors and they are thereafter called by a different name from ordinary men. Everyone has confidence in them, and sometimes witnesses are called from this class of men. Their law is, every able man must go and God will provide for his family and afterward he will be rich. Everyone who refuses to go is not a true Moslem and does not love his religion.

Preparations for the journey are made by fasting and prayer. They must repent of every sin, and sometimes one sees men praying in various ways and it is easy to see that they are preparing for a pilgrimage. They put on a sorrowful countenance and walk about sadly, all of which is merely for vain glory. Every day they must wash and cleanse themselves and go to the mosque. If they are at enmity with any one they must first be reconciled before their journey will be recognized. Some days before starting some Say-yids will ride on blue horses with long spears in their hands. They will walk in the streets crying in a loud voice to all those who are to make a pilgrimage to prepare themselves and be ready on a certain day. Together with this command are uttered words of comfort and encouragement. They tell the people not to fear; God will send, for the sake of Mohammed, His angels and prophets riding on blue horses, to deliver them from all robbers and thieves.

One month before starting each man must make donations to the poor, according to his ability. The pilgrim goes to the leader to inquire what is necessary for him to do, and how to do it, that his pilgrimage may be accepted. The priest will say, if the man is rich: "You found a mosque." If a man is poor, a small amount of money is required. Those who make their pilgrimage on horseback scatter money on the way for the benefit of the beggars and the poor. As the pilgrim sets out he is accompanied by friends for some distance, as a mark of honor to the faithful Islam. Before the band of pilgrims the leader rides, calling out in a loud voice, "Salawat." Not only the living, but also the dead shall go to these places.

Sometimes when a stingy man dies who has not gone on a pilgrimage in his lifetime, he exacts a promise from his relatives that a certain amount of his money will be used to carry his body to the holy city. If this promise is not kept, the priest will compel his relatives and heirs to restore the specified money for sacred purposes. Thus one may see caravans with hundreds, even thousands of horses with the boxes containing corpses strapped to their backs, on their way to the holy places.

When Death knocks at any door, the house is the scene of the wildest demonstrations of grief. Frequently the stillness of night is disturbed by the professional mourners. The near relatives tear their hair, scratch their faces, put on them mud and dirt, and often embrace the lifeless body.

Among the Moslems a death is announced by the Mollah from the housetop of the dead, by repeating certain portions of the Koran, and in the case of a wealthy man or a noble this is done twice. The news of death is not sent to distant friends, even if it be children, parents or brothers, as there is no one who would be the bearer or sender of such sad news. The burial follows rapidly, and in some cases people have been buried alive, as the passers by the cemeteries have heard voices, and when the graves have been opened it was found that the body had changed from the position it was placed in.

The body is taken first to a corpse-washing house, located in close proximity to a morgue, or in his own house, where it is thoroughly washed with soap and water by a professional body-washer, who is accustomed to take a suit of the dead man's clothes for his pay. It is then rinsed with abundance of fresh water, after which water containing camphor and spices is poured on the head three times, then often the entire body the same number of times, as a religious ceremony. A new white shroud is put on and wound around the body, completely covering it from head to foot. It is then placed on a bier and carried to the mosque, where it is deposited with the head pointing towards Mecca. The procession consists only of men headed by a Mollah, who repeats passages from the Koran on the way. Children's corpses are carried on a pillow and adults' on a bier. They are carried by different companies of men, who change every few minutes, as there is a merit obtained in helping.

Two priests and the friends take such a position as to face Mecca. Then the whole company rattles off the Moslem prayer in Arabic, after which the body is carried to the cemetery. It is then taken off the bier and laid alongside the selected grave, as they bury without a coffin. In the meantime prayers are said and the body is lowered and laid on its right side, the face made bare and facing Mecca. A priest takes his place at the head and in a loud voice recites in Arabic, the other Mollahs continuing their prayers. When the man at the head of the grave begins reciting, the grave digger takes the left arm of the corpse and shakes it gently till the recitation is finished, in order to attract its attention to what the Mollah has to say. The grave is roofed over with stone about a foot and a half from the bottom, thus leaving the body in a small underground enclosure. They will also paint his or her face so they will look pretty, and fill the eyes and ears and the spaces between the fingers and toes with cotton, to keep the devil away from the body. After the body is put in the ground the relatives take candies and fruits to those who attended the service, and the priest, after all are gone, will sprinkle the grave with holy water and will say to him who has died: "Give good answer to God and do not be ashamed, neither be thou afraid, because Mohammed is before God and is making intercession for you."

They believe that, after all have gone away, he will arise and will wash his face in the holy water sprinkled on his grave, and will then be ready for judgment.

Each Friday the Koran must be read at the tombs or graves of the dead. The friends and relatives will induce some one to go there and read the Koran every Friday. In this case, several families may join together to obtain a man to go and read the Koran every Friday for some hours.

Then after seven years or more, the bones will be dug out and put in boxes and prepared to be sent to Mohammed's burying ground. The object of these trips is to secure heaven for the dead, because the prophet said, "If the bones of a man should be near to mine, there will be no doubt of their resurrection with me on the last day; but if they are too far from my burying ground, then my power might not reach them, in giving them privilege of resurrection." Thus the people will do all in their power to send the bones of their beloved ones near to his burying grounds.

SOCIAL AND DOMESTIC LIFE IN PERSIA.

The birth of a child is usually awaited with a great deal of agonizing anxiety. At the announcement of the birth of a baby boy, the servants have a glorious time. They joyfully take the tidings to their master, from whom they are certain to receive gifts and hear good words. The congratulations of friends and relations will begin to pour in from all quarters to the happy father, and it will be an occasion for rejoicing and festivity. The father will deem it a privilege to entertain his friends as an expression of his personal gratification. Noise, festivity and music will fill the atmosphere with the echoes of a merry company. Everybody is happy because a son is born, one who will succeed the father, keep up the family record and perpetuate the memory of the race.

But when a daughter is born there will be no giving of gifts, no festivity, no music and no entertainments. Everybody about the house, the very atmosphere will be doleful and gloomy, as though the mourning over the loss of a precious child was already begun. The servants dread to take the tidings to their master, realizing the disappointment that will follow. When the father hears the message he will be in a woeful condition. Taking his pipe he will engage in an endless puffing, as though thus to mitigate his sorrow. The poor mother's grief is most sincere and pitiful. She weeps bitterly when her friends come to her, appreciating her situation. They address her with comforting words and encouraging prospects.

Both mother and infant will be the objects of hatred to the cruel father and the rest of the family. No word of comfort will be given to her by them. No kiss of affectionate love and no help in the time of pain and sorrow.

It is the custom for the friends of the married couple on the wedding day to sincerely express their good wishes by repeating the common saying, "May your wedded life be long and peaceful with many sons and no daughters."

The child is salted in the day she is born according to an ancient custom and subjected to the superstitions so carefully practiced among the women. If it is a boy no one can see his face for at least three months because the little thing is so precious that peradventure any one looking on him he might die.

A talisman will soon be brought, on which are written prayers and verses from the Koran. This is to be fastened on the right arm or put somewhere near the body to preserve him from sickness and especially the evil eye.

No mother allows anyone to praise her baby boy; will usually dress him in unbecoming clothes and keep him dirty, fearing if he should look too handsome and attractive, the evil eye might cause his death or illness; she will, however, do all that is in her power to make him comfortable. When he cries she is ready to rock him to sleep, singing the sweetest baby songs in his ears, and kissing his precious cheek because he is a son and a precious gift of God. But the unfortunate little daughter will have no more attention than the domestic animal at first. At the end of seven days she will be put into a hard cradle, wrapped tightly in swaddling clothing. Sometimes she will not be moved for a whole day or night, and when she is removed it will be only for a little while. When she cries the mother is slow to attend to her, and at best the only thing the mothers do for them when they cry is to rock them in the rough cradle, which does not add much to their comfort, nor soothe them into silence. After a considerable amount of singing and harsh speaking most likely the mother will get angry and tired and leave the little creature alone to cry until it can cry no more because utterly exhausted. They bind the eyes of a child very tightly with a handkerchief for the first ten or fifteen days; this they suppose protects them from nervousness caused by seeing the light for the first time. Again they never take the girls out of doors for the first forty days and the boys for three months because they believe illness will be caused by the expression of surprise from the people that see them for the first time. Again their eyes must be always filled with black powder, which they think keeps them from becoming sore and makes them pretty when they are grown.

As circumcision is practiced among the Mohammedans, boys receive their names at the celebration of this rite, at the eighth day. But at the naming of the girl, there is no religious ceremony, and no reading from the Koran or even praying by the mollah. An old woman will be called to the house, who will take the girl in her arms, and, placing her mouth to the child's ear, will call the name that her parents prefer in a very loud voice, repeating it three times, adding, " This is your name." At the age of 6, they will be put to work at home to help their mothers, and at the same time to learn what will be useful to themselves. They are taught sweeping, washing, cooking, making tea and preparing " kalaan," the water pipe, for the guests and parents; and they will be expected to give good attention to all kinds of housework. They will also be taught sewing, which is supposed to be the crowning attainment of any girl. They learn to do the most beautiful embroidery and handwork, for which the Persian women have always been famous, and this is about all the preparation they can make for their future life as a married woman.

All education is confined to the male sex only, and very seldom to the female, who might be the daughters of prominent lords and men. The customs that require the strict seclusion of females, prevents them attending school, consequently only a few wealthy families will supply special tutors for their daughters. This teacher generally is a mollah, who is a pious man, a very old man and nearly blind. As these blind mollahs know the Koran by heart, they make very good teachers. He will be permitted to go to the women's apartment in the house and take a seat at one end of the room, while the pupil sits at the other; some elderly women will be present, while the teacher drills the pupils in reading the Koran and explains its teachings to them.

The common age of betrothal for a girl is between the ages of 7 and 12 – very seldom over that age : but in many cases a girl is betrothed as soon as she is born, or even before her birth. I have known certain parties who were friends before their marriage, while sitting together socially drinking, that one suggested to make a contract between them that, after they were married, if one had a son and the other a daughter, they would marry them — and the contract was fulfilled perfectly ; at present the young man is dead, but the young lady is still living. In some places in the Kurdistan Mountains, the engagement will take place as soon as a girl is born; and in such cases they will take the girl in their home and care, and bring her up. The engagement ceremony will take place by first sending a private message to the girl's father, indicating their wishes. If the father favors the idea, the messenger will return with words of encouragement, and then the date of ceremony will be fixed. Then the father of the boy, taking a few relatives with him, with a ring and a pair of shoes, etc. and a great deal of candy and some other confectionery, goes to the home of the girl. After an elaborate salutation, they will be given seats and a general conversation will take place for about an hour, after which the father of the boy will mention the object of his coming, addressing the family with a few polite and appropriate words. The father of the girl, who is expected to decide the matter, at first will make no definite answer, but will say, "The girl does not belong to me, she has a grandfather who must be consulted first "; and then the grandfather will be addressed, and pressed for a definite answer. After a few moments of silence he will place the matter before the girl's uncle, and so it will go the rounds of all the nearest relatives, each one being consulted in turn, just for the sake of ceremony and to make them feel good. At last, the question comes back to the girl's father for a definite answer, and he will say, gravely, "My daughter is like a pair of shoes for your son." That means, I am willing to make the engagement. Then it is the duty of the boy's father to kiss the hand of every relative of the girl who is present. Meantime, the ring will be carried to the ladies' apartment, where the girl is, and handed to the girl by an elderly woman, who, addressing her, will say, "Your father, your uncles and your brother have betrothed you to ———, and if you are willing to obey them, you can express it by taking this ring from my hand and putting it on your finger"; and the girl is always expected to do it—but I know of a case where a girl's desire was for another young man, and did refuse the ring, and then her uncle went there with a dagger in one hand and the ring in the other and said, "Choose the ring or the dagger," and she chose the ring. Then the presents will be offered to the girl, and the feast will be continued until late in the night. Thus the engagement is completed.

The duration of the engagement varies greatly; some marry after six months, others more or less, and it even continues for five or six years. But the boy and girl have very little to say concerning the engagement; in many cases they are too young to understand the meaning of it. There is no calling upon their sweethearts, or walking with them, nor are they together in society. It is improper for a girl to allow her sweetheart to see her, as the love of a Mussulman is measured largely by the beauty of a woman. A boy is naturally very anxious to see his future wife, and will often watch eagerly to meet her or have a word with her.

The old women, who play an important part in these affairs, are always ready to stimulate a curiosity of either party by pointing out one to the other. Once or twice during the engagement the young man will be given a half hour's intercourse with his sweetheart, but it must be in the presence of an elderly woman.

One of the special features of Persian weddings is the extravagance. From the time the engagement takes place until the wedding is over large sums of money are being spent continually by both parties, more especially by the bridegroom's family. The wealthy may not feel the pressure much, but there are some upon whom it brings a heavy burden of debt for life. Still they think it necessary because a man's character and generosity are judged by the style in which he marries his son.

The greatest expense is what is called "parcha," the wedding garments. A few weeks before the wedding takes place both parties will send their representatives, and they will be engaged for one, two or three days in making purchases. Usually they buy from three to seven different suits for the bride, giving but small attention to the bridegroom's apparel, as he is expected to see after his own. As the expenses must all be paid by the boy's father, the bride's party is naturally inclined to be lavish, while the other party, in seeking to modify their desires, often raise quarrels of ill-feeling. The expenditure sometimes amounts to hundreds of dollars, among the wealthy. When the "parcha" is taken to the bride's home all the maidens from the neighborhood get together and help cut out and sew. Of course the larger part must be done by herself, if she is old enough to understand dressmaking, and by her mother. Very few people employ dressmakers on such occasions.

A day or two before the wedding the bridegroom's people will despatch two or three men to the villages and towns of the neighborhood to invite all the friends, relations and respectable citizens. They carry with them candy and red apples, which are to take the place of the engraved cards. Handing a red apple or some candy to the family, they announce verbally the day of the wedding, adding these words: "So-and-so sends his love to you and to your family and says, the wedding is not my son's, but yours; come and bring your family." Then, bidding them farewell, they will go to the next neighbor and repeat the same thing until their mission is fulfilled. If there is a grandee or official connected with either family, the boy's father has to go himself, carrying a sheep or a quantity of sweets, and extend the invitation to him. In return he will receive the gift of a shawl or tailor-made coat for the bridegroom, with his excellency's good wishes and permission to proceed with the ceremony.

It will be interesting to mention that it sometimes occurs that some of those invited, from pique or ill-humor, will decline to attend the wedding; then the father of the boy will go himself or send a near relative to pacify them and persuade them to come to the feast The weddings generally last from three to seven days.

On the first day the invited guests will pour into the home of the bridegroom, which will be opened for their cordial reception. Everybody makes himself at home. Dancing, music, noisy drums and the uncontrollable excitement of the merry crowd will fill the air the whole of the seven days. The first three or four days are usually spent in feasting at the bridegroom's, while the bride's family are quietly going on with their preparations for their daughter. The principal part of the entertainments on these days is eating. The home will be thrown open for not only the guests, but for all the poor people and the beggars. Sometimes from five to ten sheep will be slain, or one or two oxen. Quantit.es of rice and other vegetables will be used. Three times every day this crowd of people will sit on the floor around the long tables to eat, of course with their fingers according to the custom of the country.

Dancing—Between meals they will go out to the open court, which is like an amphitheater, or if that is not large enough, out on the street to engage in dancing and singing, the women and children crowding the flat roofs of that house and neighboring ones to look at the dancers. The men hand in hand form a large circle, the one at the head, the leader, holding a richly colored handkerchief in one hand, and swinging it in the air, moves slowly around, the others following, while the drummer and flute player stand in the center of the circle making a violent noise. Gradually they begin to get excited and become more and more so until they jump and leap so rapidly that their feet can hardly be seen at all. When one is tired another takes his place in the circle, and thus they go on till noon. Sometimes a drum and flute will be exchanged for two good singers who sing love songs for the inspiration of the dancers. The women are not allowed to dance with the gentlemen. They can dance in their own apartments or when there are no strangers present. It is customary for each neighbor who is present at the supper table and meets with the strangers there to take from two to five of them home with him when the time for retiring comes and take care of them for the night. Thus lodgings are provided for a great many. Sometimes there will be none left at the bridegroom's house. Then early in the morning the drummers go about the street and summon them back for their breakfast.

On the third or fourth day they arrange to go after the bride. Some thirty or forty of the choicest young men, well dressed and armed, and if the bride's home be at some distance some of them mounted on beautiful horses march toward the house, where they will receive a cordial welcome. Everything has been prepared for their reception, the village people will come, and the feasting will begin at the home of the bride. The bride's family generally look rather doleful during this part of the performance, probably on account of the expense. The next morning the bride will be gorgeously decked in her wedding apparel in the women's apartment, a red veil taking the place of the black one for the day and covering the whole of her body. She is not allowed even to have the small openings to see through. Bidding her folks goodbye, she is put upon a horse saddled for her, and at this point begins a tremendous uproar from the crowd—yells, shouts, thundering of guns, etc. The bride is carefully protected from every danger by three men, a "koolam" servant holding the bridle and leading the horse and the other two holding her, one on either side. Thus the homeward march begins. Each one of the young men belonging to the bride's escort carries a chicken in his hand which either he catches himself from the street or some friend catches and gives to him. This is called the bridegroom's bird. The procession advances as rapidly as possible. The city people often have these processions at night so that they can have the opportunity to make them more resplendent by fireworks, that is, by torches, etc.

It was on such an occasion that the parable of the ten virgins was suggested to the Master. When they are near home a messenger is dispatched to carry the news of their approach to the bridegroom. For this he will receive some reward. The bridegroom then dresses himself in his wedding costume and, attended by his intimate companions, he goes out of his chamber looking as happy and gorgeous as the sun coming out of the chambers of the night. This part of the ceremony differs a good deal in various parts of the country. In some places, the bridegroom and his staff just go a little distance to meet the bride. In other places, he

CARRYING WATER.
REAPERS. (Page 134.

CHRISTIAN PERSIAN MOTHER AT THE SIDE OF THE CRADLE.

goes out on top of the roof and waits until the bride arrives in sight. Her horse will be led through the multitude to a corner of the street directly opposite the bridegroom; then he will shoot her with three red apples. Occasionally he aims too accurately and the poor little bride is struck and probably hurt by the red apples. Each shooting of an apple is greeted by loud yelling of the excited crowd. In some places it is customary to take the bride to the doors of the prominent people of the place and nearest relations, before going to her father-in-law's. This is considered a mark of respect to such persons, and at each home the family is expected to show their appreciation in some way. Some take a quantity of raisins and throw them upon her head, as a symbol of the "sweetness of the occasion," while others throw a great deal of copper money, a symbol of prosperity. The boys especially enjoy this part of the performance and have a great time picking up the raisins and coppers under the horses' feet. After this they proceed to the bridegroom's house and everybody will retire until the next morning, when dancing and feasting begin again. The main feature of the next day's proceedings will be the welcoming of the bride's relatives and friends, who will come and bring her trunk and all that belongs to her. Her trunk must be opened before a multitude of witnesses and every little thing in it spread out before them. The contents of this trunk are not, by any means, entirely for the bride's own use, although she and her mother have spent a great deal of time on them. They are mostly intended as presents for the bridegroom's relations and friends, and are the greatest expense which falls on her father in connection with the wedding days. In the trunk there will be perhaps some half a dozen or more dresses, aprons, skirts, head-dresses, etc., made for her by her parents; the rest are all the presents that have been made, consisting of side-pockets, waist-pockets, money bags, watch covers, woolen belts, skull caps and such like, all of which have been exquisitely embroidered by hand. These will be distributed among the numerous relation and home-folk of the bridegroom.

If the bride's father is wealthy the trunk will also contain jewels, precious stones, shawls, cups of gold and silver; a "samowar," or teakettle, with all its outfit; a "kalean," smoking pipe, etc. It will be as well to remark that these costly gifts, in many cases, are not so much for the purpose of expressing the parents' devotion to the daughter as for the show and pride on their own behalf.

On the next day the guests will begin to depart. In leaving, everyone extends his congratulation and presents his gift. This ends the wedding. The married couple, instead of taking a bridal trip to some land or city, will remain at home, rarely going out at all for two or three months.

THE DWELLING PLACE OF A MARRIED WOMAN.

The Persians have a strong tendency to congregate in cities, towns and villages, from the rich capitalists and the high officials to the poor laboring men and peasants. They all prefer to live together in communities. There is literally none of what is called country life in America. Most of the cities, towns and villages have high, thick walls of mud all around them, with gates for entrance, which are carefully watched. The reason for this is, I suppose, first, for protection in time of war. In the olden days the country was settled largely by different hostile tribes who would often attack each other, and the walls were a great protection to the property. There were also numerous robbers and highwaymen whose whole business was thieving and pillage, thus constantly dangerous to life and commerce.

There is still this danger, and the citizens to insure their safety live in communities for mutual defense and protection. And, again, the custom of secluding the women has a great deal to do with it.

The first visible part of the houses of the first class from the street is a high, thick wall that encircles the whole lot. Through this there is only one entrance—a large gate, made of heavy hard wood and studded with big, heavy iron nails. This gate is kept shut all the time, and anybody that wanted to get in would have to knock hard in order to do so, calling the family, who, in most cases, live in some distant part of the premises. Walking along the street, one can easily tell the official house, because they have always about a dozen or more men guarding the gate. These guards eat, sleep and live in the small rooms opening into the gateway on each side. No neighbor is allowed to build his house higher than the mud walls, or if he does, he is not permitted to open any window— not the least open-ing—into his neighbor's yard which could make it pos-sible for him to look in upon his neighbor's wife.

The first apartment we come to is called "beroon," or the men's apartment. Here the head of the family during the day commands his servants, transacts his business and receives his calls. He comes to this apart-ment by sunrise, having previously had his cup of coffee or tea and offered his prayers. And here he stays until his dinner hour, which is at twilight. The second apart-ment of the house is called "anderoon," which is exclu-sively for women and children, and is also called "harem," "forbidden place," a word corresponding with zenana or serago. The women live here all their lives, very sel-dom going out for recreation or a breath of fresh air. No male persons could venture to go to this apartment. If a man by mistake or unwittingly should attempt to make his way to the "forbidden place," he would be quickly met by the guardians and eunuchs, crying loudly, "Women, away!" and the man, with breathless haste, will make his way back, while the women would begin at once to conceal their persons with a veil.

The custom of secluding the women and watching them so carefully has come down from many generations. The kings in ancient days, in order to exhibit greater state and to preserve pure lineage, introduced it first into the country, and it was gradually adopted in some form by all classes, except the wandering nomads.

Duties of Women in Persia.

One of the duties of women in Persia is grinding the wheat and barley into flour. In the parts of the country where water is abundant, water mills are built, and in some other places they have what are called donkey, buffalo or mule mills, which are turned by power of these animals. But still there are many of the poor who cannot afford to have their flour ground at these mills, and the women must grind it at home in the old fashioned way of Bible lands and times. "Two women shall be grinding at the mill: the one shall be taken and the other left." (Matt. 24, 41). This mill consists of two heavy circular stones with a wooden pin in the center fastened to the lower one passing through a large hole in the upper one. Into this hole in the upper stone, around the central pin, the grain is poured by handfuls while the two women turn it rapidly by the stout handle fastened to the outer rim of the upper stone. The grain falling between the two stones is crushed into a coarse flour and thrown out around the edges onto a large cloth placed under and around the mill for the purpose of catching it.* Besides the flour for the bread they prepare every year a quantity of cracked wheat, which is boiled and dried in small cakes from which they make a much relished dish peculiar to the Persian poorer classes. The bread is made up with leaven, worked and set to rise, then rolled out into very thin cakes. A second woman has in her hand a kind of cushion covered with heavy canvas. The thin wafer of dough is spread smoothly on this cushion, which has a handle underneath so that she can hold it securely. Then she slaps the cake of dough against the hot side of the tandoor (oven) so that it sticks and bakes in a few minutes, when another is put in its place. A week's baking, sometimes two weeks', is done at once.

Water works have not been introduced into Persia yet; all the water for drinking and every day use is brought from a distance by the women. There are public wells or streams outside of each village. The women go to these places mornings and evenings and carry home as much as is needed. If it is a well they have no pumps, so they have to pull it up in an earthen vessel with a long rope and fill their jars from that, but if it is a spring they simply plunge the jar in until full, then lift it, first on the hip, then to the back or shoulder, and quickly march home. They go back and forth this way until all their jars are full, sometimes eight or ten times. The jars are large and heavy, made of earthenware. They hold from five to eight gallons of water. It takes long practice and strong arms to lift these jars to the shoulder without spilling any of the water or dropping and breaking the jar. But these women who have been accustomed to the exercise need no dumb-bells or skipping ropes for the development of their muscles. It is a beautiful sight every morning and night when scores of women group together with their jars upon their backs and march to the spring. They find some compensation for the laborious task in the freedom to gossip and talk along the way, and look as if they really enjoy it. It reminds one of the romantic story of Abraham's servant and Rebecca at the well

(Gen, 24) and of the more spiritual incident of our Savior and the woman of Samaria at Jacob's well.*

The churning is done in a large, oddly shaped earthen jar, laid upon its side on what is called a saddle. That is a kind of hollowed bridge, into which the jar fits and over which it is jolted back and forth, to make the butter come. First, however, the fresh milk is boiled and a little sour cream or butter-milk added. Then it is allowed to stand until it has become perfectly solid. The mouth of the jar is then tied up tight with a heavy piece of canvas, that no air can get in, and the jolting begins. Gathering the butter, etc., is similar to the same process in America.*

Most of the harvesting, also, is done by women. It usually begins in the early part of June and lasts until the latter part of July or the first of August. These months are very hard on the women. They have to be up early in order to finish their domestic duties by an hour after sunrise. Then they take sickles and march to the field, which is usually from one to two miles distant. Often one sees a mother with her infant in a cradle upon her shoulder and a sickle in her hand marching with the rest. From morning until sunset they toil, with only two hours for rest in the middle of the day. The mothers put the baby-cradle under a tree, where they can see that no harm comes to the little one, and can stop and rock it if it cries very hard. These harvest months are the very hottest in the year. The sun shines with terrific force during the day. While the women reap, the men gather up the bundles and bind them ready to be carried to the threshing floor, which is a great distance from the field. Many a poor "Ruth" may be seen following the reapers, gleaning whatever may fall behind. At sunset they begin their homeward journey, tired and dirty.* Their home duties are to come afterward, before they are ready to rest.

By the time the harvest is over, the vineyard work begins. The grapes are then ripe. The women pick the ripe and ready bunches, filling large baskets and carrying them to the end of the vineyard, where they are spread out in the sun to be dried for raisins. This usually takes from fifteen to twenty days. Then they gather them and pile them up at home, ready for the market. The rest of the grapes are made into molasses and wine. Of course the men take some part in the vineyard work, but most of it is done by the women.

When a husband eats, the wife cannot sit with him and eat at the same table, but must always stand in his presence with her arms crossed while he eats, ready to render any service to him, like an accomplished slave. And after he has done eating, she pours water on her lord's hands, and wipes them on a towel or her own chader; then she lights his water-pipe and with a graceful yet slavish bow she hands it to him; and while he enjoys it she serves the children in the same fashion, after which she retires to a respectful distance, her face turned toward the black mud walls, so that her lord may not see her lips moving, and finishes the meal. When he walks on the street, she cannot walk anywhere near him, because it is a reproach for a man to be seen on the street with a woman, and also because she is so covered with the out-door costume. He might be accused of walking with a woman who was not his wife. Hence, she never expects any help or protection from him. When he goes on a journey, he does not even tell her good-bye, or consult with her about his trip; and if he should be gone for years, would never write her a single letter nor ask after her health. If anything needs to be attended to, he writes to his brothers or father, or a near relative. Nor does he ever trust his wife with any money for her living; he will ask a friend or relative to give it to her little by little. When he is in any business trouble or perplexity, it will not occur to him to mention the fact to her or to ask her advice. On the contrary, when he talks business with his friends she must not listen. And if she were in any mental or physical depression, she would not dare mention it to him, for she would be sure of harsh, rough words, instead of loving sympathy. In all these things, he is in no sense a husband to her, but only a lord and owner.

The law requires that females also make pilgrimages to the holy places. Girls at every age are allowed to go; also children. Widows under 50 years are not accepted as pilgrims, first, because of their probable desire for marriage, and second, because the law says no women must undertake a pilgrimage alone for fear of exposing themselves to men. So, in order to go, some marry for this purpose. The husband accompanies them thither, and upon returning either divorces them or keeps them as wives or concubines.

Every band of pilgrims, when returning to their own city, will send a messenger about ten days in advance to announce that in so many days a band of pilgrims will appear in the city. On the day of their arrival many hundred men will meet them several miles from the city. The Say-yids ride before them, crying: "Salawats!" Friends and relatives kill lambs as a sacrifice before them. This sacrifice is a holy matter and no man can touch it till its blood is shed; but when it is beheaded it belongs to God, and the strongest man takes it for his own. So there is always quarreling when the pilgrims return. The acquaintances of the pilgrims will come and say: "My portion be as thy portion. Blessed art thou. May your pilgrimage be accepted." And the pilgrim will answer: "God grant that you may also go to this Holy Place and receive remission of sins." Women will sometimes cut pieces

from the pilgrims' garments, which are supposed to be
holy. At the pilgrim's home many sheep are killed and
a variety of fine meats are cooked. People gather there
to eat and drink and they say to the host: "God bless
your pilgrimage." He will answer: "May the Prophet
give you success and grant that you too may visit the
Holy Place."

LIFE OF MOHAMMED AND MOHAMMEDISM.

Mohammed was born at Mecca in the year 570. He
was from the tribe of Koreish. His great-grandfather
was married to a lady of Medina and Mohammed was
thus connected with one of the ruling families of that
city—the Bani Khazraj. Abdallah, his father, was
poor, and died on a mercantile trip to Syria shortly before Mohammed's birth. His mother, Amina, according
to the custom of Mecca, put the infant out to nurse with
a Bedouin tribe; and there the child remained for four
or five years, acquiring the free habits and the pure
tongue of the nomad race.

About a year after Amina took the lad to visit his
relatives at Medina, but on the way home she died, so
that in his sixth year Mohammed was left an orphan.
His uncle, Abu Taleb, became his guardian and to the
day of his death faithfully discharged the trust. While
yet a child Mohammed accompanied his uncle to Syria
on a mercantile journey, where he came in contact with
a number of Christians and Jews, from whom he learned
much about the Jewish and Christian principles of
religion. His uncle procured for him the commission
from a rich widow to superintend a trading caravan to
Syria. Khadija, delighted with her agent's service,
conceived a tender passion for him, and though nearly
40, while he was but 25 years of age, became his wife.
She bore him two sons and four daughters. Both sons

died. The eldest, who survived two years, was called Kasim; whence Mohammed's name of Abul Kasim.

At the age of 40 a new life was quickened in the soul of Mohammed, who claimed that he received a revelation from God. An angel appeared to him and in mortal terror Mohammed ran to his wife and cried, "Wrap me up!" and he lay wrapped up in his cloak.

The angel said :—

O thou covered! Rise up and warn!
And thy Lord magnify!
And thy garments purify!
And abomination shun!
And grant not favors to gain increase!
And the Lord await!

Revelation after revelation followed in rapid succession. He did not doubt his mission. His first converts were among his own family and kinsmen—his wife, daughters, cousin Ali, and his freedman, Zaid.

At first Mohammed attracted little attention at Mecca, but soon after his claim of being the prophet of God was known, and especially when he spoke against idolatry, they persecuted him and his enemies violently tried to kill him, but he fled from Mecca to Medina. (The day of his flight marks the year of Hegira or Emigration, A. D. 622. This is the beginning of the Mohammedan era.)

In Medina Mohammed built a mosque. After he had a number of followers he declared the Holy War, by which he succeeded in conquering many tribes and countries. Then, two years later, he returned to Mecca at the head of a great army and conquered it. He then returned to his home and died in Medina, 632 A. D. Over his burial-place a large mosque has since been built. After his death his successor took his place and extended his mission through Persia, Babylonia, Syria, Asia Minor, Egypt and Spain. In the course of one hundred and ten years they had met with great and wonderful success. Of course this was due to the means which they used, viz: the sword.

This religion was introduced in Spain with the intention of carrying it on through Europe. Now, what was it that prevented them from doing this? The Christians who had heard about the Mohammedans and their intentions gathered together their armies under the direction of Charles Martel and went to meet the Saracens. It was at the battle of Tours, 732 years after Christ, or 110 years after Mohammed had started on his mission, that these two great powers met. Thus there was a great struggle between the Mohammedans and Christians, between the false and true religions. In this battle the Mohammedans were defeated and gave up their intentions. A few years later they were driven out of Spain, and ever since have not had any accession to the powers of the world that they did not control at that time.

The total number of the Mohammedans throughout the whole world is 175,000,000. These are in Africa, Turkey, Persia, Afghanistan, Beloochistan, India, Ceylon. Their belief is that there is one God, Mohammed is his apostle, and the Koran a sacred book.

The first doctrine which we meet in the Mohammedan creed is this: "LA ILAHA ILLA 'LLAHU MUHAMMADUN RASULU LLAHI." "There is no God but God: Mohammed is the prophet of God." Mohammedans ascribe ninety-nine names or titles to God, among which some of the principal are, the Merciful, the Gracious, the Master, the Holy, the Creator, the Faithful, the Pardoner, the Wrathful, the Provider of daily bread, the All-wise, the Just, the King, the Great, the Exalter, the Glorious, the Lover, the Witness, the Truth, the Almighty, the First, the Last, the Pure, the Light, the Guide, the Patient One, etc. Mohammed taught that

God, most high, created the seven days of the week; on Sunday He created the gates of the highest heaven; on Monday the seven stories of heaven; on Tuesday He constructed the seven stories of the earth; on Wednesday He made darkness; on Thursday He created the produce of the earth and all that is in it; on Friday He made the sun, moon and stars, and caused the seven celestial spheres to revolve; and on the sixth day He created the whole world. One day, however, of that upper world is said to be equal to one thousand years.

One day while Mohammed was talking with some of his followers the archangel Gabriel appeared to them in disguise of a very tall and strong man clothed in white, who for their information and instruction said to the prophet: "O, Mohammed, tell me about Islam." Mohammed replied: "Islam is that thou shalt bear witness, that there is no God but God and that Mohammed is the apostle of God; second, to offer five prayers each day; third, to give alms; fourth, to perform pilgrimages to Mecca; fifth, to fast during Ramazan." The angel continued: "I accept this as true. Now tell me about faith." Mohammed said: "It is to believe in God and his angels and in his books and in his messenger; in the last day and in fate regarding good and evil." The angel replied: "I accept this also as true; now tell me about well doing." Mohammed answered: "It is to serve God as if thou didst see Him, even though thou see Him not, for indeed He seeth thee."

Mohammedans hold, that from the very beginning God taught his servants by direct inspiration, that Adam, Enoch, Noah, Abraham, Moses and Jesus, as well as a multitude of the prophets, were sent by Him as occasion required; some for all men and some for individual tribes, that they might guide men to God and reveal His will.

The number of books which have been revealed to the prophets is 103. Out of this number ten were intrusted to Adam, fifty to Seth, thirty to Abraham, ten to Moses, one to David, one to Jesus and one to Mohammed, and they believe when one revelation became lost or corrupted a new message was sent down. The last of all the prophets, according to them, is Mohammed, and hence the final and most perfect revelation is that contained in the Koran, and they hold that it is incumbent upon all men, therefore, to accept their creed or they will be cast into the eternal punishment. Mohammedans believe that the entire Koran was dictated to Mohammed by Gabriel, and is a literal copy of what was written ages before the creation of the world by divine decree upon the everlasting tablet in heaven. With regard to creation of man the Mohammedans believe that Adam was created in a garden in heaven; but God sent an angel to obtain a handful of earth, of which the body of Adam was then made. When the spirit entered this body God ordered all the angels to worship Adam. All obeyed except Iblis, who was thereupon condemned to hell-fire and became known as Satan. Eve was created from Adam's rib, and when they ate of the forbidden fruit, which they hold was wheat, they were cast down from the heavenly paradise and fell to the earth. When Adam fell, he kept on weeping for his offence for three hundred years, so that from his tears rivers began to flow and on their banks there grew dates and nut trees. Every tear of Eve, which fell into the sea, became a pearl and diamond, and then God commanded Adam to make pilgrimage to Mecca and there he met Eve and recognized her because during the fall Eve was cast in one direction and Adam another

The doctrine of original sin finds no place in Mohammedan theology, although they hold that all men are descendants of Adam and Eve—that Adam did not sin, but simply erred. They believe in the multitudinous existence of the angels, as having all been created ages before creation by God, from fire, and being superior, therefore, to man. They are, however, capable of falling into sin, and are appointed to various offices; are of different rank, and God uses many of them as messengers to mankind. In the highest rank are those nearest to God; these are the four supporters of His throne. On the judgment day four more will be appointed to this service, because it is written in the Koran that the eight angels will support the throne of God on the last day. An angel predominates in hell, and under his authority are nineteen others, appointed to aid him in maintaining authority. They are preserved from being injured by the flames, as they have a seal of divinity impressed upon their foreheads, with the inscription, "There is no god but God; Mohammed is the apostle of God."

Five times a day there is a solemn call which sounds forth from the mosque to prayer in these words: "Assahu Akbar!" (God is most great) repeated four times in a loud tone of voice, then in a lower tone. The caller says, repeating each clause separately twice, "I bear witness that there is no God but God; I bear witness that Mohammed is the apostle of God." Then raising his voice once more, he again recites these two clauses twice, and then proceeding in the same tone he cries, "Come to prayer, come to prayer! Come to the refuge, come to the refuge!" God is most great, God is most great! There is no god but God!" In the morning call, he adds: "Prayer is better than sleep."

They pray five times a day—in the morning before sun-rise, at noon, before sun-set, during the twilight, after sunset, when night has commenced. At these specified times Mussulmen, wherever they may be, in the street or in the house, spread their rugs out upon the ground and, facing Mecca, recite the set form of prayer in Arabic, claiming that to be the language of paradise.

The prophet commanded that the children should be directed to offer the appointed prayers at the age of 7 and that they should be beaten if they fail to comply. The public prayers in the Mosque are conducted by a priest or leader, who turns his face toward Mecca. Behind him rank after rank stand on a spot which is marked out for the worshiper, space enough for each to enable him to prostrate himself. Before a man spreads his rug, he takes off his shoes, carefully performs the ceremony of washing his hands and ears and face, water being always near at hand. In case there is no water, sand is used. They all have to cross a bridge after death, the unrighteous will fall down to the lowest hell; this bridge is as thin as a hair and is sharper than a sword.

Islam teaches that God alone, the Almighty Creator and Preserver, the Master and Judge of all creation, shall be worshiped, but of God's infinite holiness and love, Mohammedism knows nothing.

The prophet, Mohammed, after visiting the seventh heaven on a night journey, entered the very presence of God himself. "In the sixth heaven," said Mohammed, "I met Moses, who asked me, 'What hast thou been commanded to do?' I answered, 'I have been commanded to teach the people to offer fifty prayers a day.' Moses replied, 'Verily, the people will not be able to comply with this request. I have tried it with Israel in the wilderness. Return thou, therefore, to thy Lord and ask of him that he lessen the burden for thy people.'" I returned and God reduced the burden by ten prayers. Then I returned to Moses, but he said as before. I went back and God again relieved me of ten prayers. I went once more to Moses, who advised me again as before. I did so and was left with but ten prayers which my people were to offer.

Then Moses advised me once more to return, which I did, and was left with five prayers, consequently their prayer is a kind of tribute to be paid to God as his due and not in any way a means of heartfelt spiritual communication with Him but rather the homage due to a Lord by his slave.

Mohammed said: "Righteousness for you is to believe in God and the last day, the angels, the books, the prophets, and give your wealth to the poor, to the beggars and to those in bondage." All Mohammedans believe that they will be saved through Mohammed's intercession. Mohammedism teaches that there is no similitude whatever between God and man, nor is it desirable that there should be. They confess that they are sinners, but by inference and conclusions from the rest of their teachings we see that they maintain the idea that God is Himself the author of all their sinful acts.

Again, from the Koran and tradition, it is evident that Mohammed regarded sin as a mere external pollution, and capable of being washed off by performance of certain rites. Five prayers are the means of wiping out the sin, to a great extent, and pilgrimage and almsgiving is needed to take away the guilt. Mohammedism teaches nothing for atonement of sin. The Sheahs generally believe that Hassan and Hussain died as their redeemers.

Tradition speaks on the subject of the reward in the next world as follows: In paradise there are palaces made of pearls. In each palace there are seventy abodes made of rubies; in each abode there are seventy houses of emerald; in every house, a harem; in every harem, seventy beds of various colors; on every bed, an houri. In every house there are seventy tables; on each table there are seventy kinds of food; in each house there are

MY BROTHER, JACOB ADAMS.

SCHOOL AT ALKAI.

seventy slave girls, and every morning when he is anxious for food the Mussulman is given all that he desires; besides, their beauty shall be as the moon in the night; their vessels and combs shall be of gold and silver. Every one of them shall have two wives. Every man among the people of paradise shall surely have 500 houries, 4,000 virgins, 8,000 divorced women, and two large-eyed houries shall sing to him with charming voices. The inhabitants of paradise have horses and camels, and there the bridles and saddles are of rubies; and if any man among the inhabitants of paradise should desire children, they shall be born to him in one single day. The people of paradise are smooth and beardless, white and curly-haired; they shall be 30 years of age, as was Adam when he was created; their height shall be sixty cubits.

If a woman of Paradise should come down to the earth she would illuminate and fill the space between heaven and earth with her perfume. The people of Paradise shall be waited upon with seventy dishes of gold, each dish shall have a different color; they shall have in addition the liver of the fish; for them shall be slaughtered the ox. The tales which Mohammed told of the delights of Paradise were equaled by the ghastly horrors with which he surrounded the future state of all who should reject his claims.

It is believed that all Mussulmen, even those guilty of the most atrocious crimes, after a period will be ultimately in some manner delivered from hell and admitted to paradise, there to enjoy various degrees of that pleasure peculiar to their carnal nature.

Prophet Mohammed told his people that the earth was originally made out of the foam of a whale which God created. The earth consists like heaven of seven stories, and the whole mass rests between the horns of a bull. This animal has no less than four thousand horns.

The distance between any two of these horns is five hundred years' journey. His feet rests upon a fish which swims in water forty years' journey deep. Koran teaches the virgin Mary is the sister of Aaron and the daughter of Amram. Certainly Islam is an anti-Christian faith, a Christless creed, and it has preserved in the life and character of its founder an enduring principle of degredation.

The Koran denies trinity, the divine sonship of our Redeemer, his atoning death, and his mediatorial office. Mohammed taught his followers that Christ had prophesied of His coming when promising the disciples the gift of the Holy Ghost. Christ Jesus tells us that God is our heavenly Father, loving, holy and just. Mohammed teaches his followers that God is our Master, arbitrary and despotic, favoring whom He will and leading astray whom He will. The Bible informs us that man was originally created in God's image, that he was once holy, but is now fallen from his true nature. Yet God loves him and has provided a way for his restoration to peace and full realization of His being the child of God. The Koran on the other hand tells us that man was created weak and that he is and always has been separated from his Creator by a great gulf; that his nature is just and ever will be. Man is in no sense a child of God, but he is a slave. We Christians believe that sin is the transgression of the eternal moral law, which is a necessary part of the divine nature, hence sin is contrary to man's original nature as a being made in God's image and likeness. Christ tells his disciples that the most tolerable of all possible kinds of doom is being left in a state of eternal sin, eternal alienation or estrangement from God and to all that is good and true and noble, and to all that is pure and unselfish. Mohammedans hold that sin is the breach of certain arbitrary rules laid down by God for man to obey. The Bible informs us that salvation consists in the deliverance from the love and power of sin and in the restoration unto our first nature, and of bringing our whole nature in harmony with God. According to Mohammedan faith salvation means escape from the punishment of sin, while their mystics would explain the word as signifying deliverance from mental ignorance regarding God. We Christians believe that redemption is to be obtained freely through the atonement wrought out for us by Christ himself. Mussulmen maintain that they will be made righteous by their works or through Mohammed's intercession, while others maintain that Hassan's and Hussein's death were the atonement for sin. We Christians look forward for an eternal happiness and for many mansions of our heavenly Father's home, where nothing that defiles can enter, but where we shall know even as we are known and shall be renewed in the image of our Creator and our Redeemer. Mohammed promised his followers a heaven of carnal delight and sensual pleasure, etc. If we believe that only through Christ can God, the Father, be properly known to us, that only through Christ's atoning death can we hope for salvation, that only through union with Him can we possess the true life which he came to give us, then it must be plain that the Mohammedan religion is entirely out of the question.

Islam as a religion is not true, it has not come from God. It does not and cannot satisfy the needs of the human heart, it does not reveal God in His Divine Fatherhood, in His love, His justice and His Holiness. It does not show man what his own original nature was, nor reveal to him what sin is and how to escape it. Islam is an anti-Christian creed. It is opposed to all true progress, whether moral or intellectual, political or religious. This being the case, then Mohammedism cannot take the place of Christianity with advantage to any section of the human race. Mohammed is in every way unfit to be an ideal of a human being. But Christianity has a duty to the Mussulman, one which we cannot shirk without incurring serious responsibility. We must not be content to leave them alone in their darkness and bigotry. If we would we cannot altogether do so, brought in contact with the great Mohammedan world as we are at the present time. If we would ask what our duty to the Mussulman is, our divine Lord gives us a very clear answer: "Go ye and make all nations disciples, baptizing them in the name of the Father, Son and Holy Ghost." Christ died for them as well as for the heathen and for ourselves, and he has his own chosen among all nations. To us is committed the ministry of reconciliation, the sacred duty of calling the followers of the Arabian anti-Christ to the foot of the cross of the crucified Redeemer whose atoning death they deny and Godhead they blaspheme.

Our duty to Mohammedans is clear and little have we Christians done or are we doing in bringing them to Christ. The work in Persia is still in its infancy and likewise in many other countries. There are yet 175,000,000 of Mohammedans. Let us each and everyone ask ourselves what we have done in delivering them from the false prophet. We are not to convert the Mohammedans, but he who has promised to be with His messengers even to the end can and doth turn the heart of many wherever the gospel is faithfully preached to them; it is not too much to say, that it is the gospel of Christ unto salvation to the Mussulman, as well as every other seeker of truth. Oh, thank God, that His word is strong and able to convict the sinner to His saving grace.

It may be interesting to know something of the method generally adopted of bringing the Gospel to bear on Mohammedans. We endeavor to convince them of their sinfulness and weakness, their need of an atonement for sin; a Redeemer who can and will deliver them, not only from its punishment, but also from its power. We invite them to search Koran and their traditions and tell us what provision they find therein to satisfy their deep need. Needless is it to say, Islam knows of no atonement and no Savior. Or again we point out the Koran's testimony to the Bible and induce them to study the holy books thus commended to all true believers. A Mohammedan, with whom I was thus reading St. John's Gospel, said to me: "If a Moslem has read the Gospel for even three days, he may still fear to become a Christian, yet he will never again believe in Mohammed."

We endeavor once again to get down to the grand truths of Christianity, to show how true these are, how very much more true than Mohammed ever suspected. We show how they were recognized by Jews and Christian ages before Mohammed, and that Islam has forgotten many similar truths and defaced those which it has retained. We induce them to get to know Christ's character and work and contrast it with those of the prophet of Arabia. Such a method never fails if pursued in a loving and prayerful spirit, to produce an effect upon the heart and conscience of any thoughtful Moslem. All such do not embrace Christianity, but it is impossible for them entirely to reject the attraction which Christ Jesus exercises, or to make Mohammed their ideal and their hope. "Some men know God," said a Moslem friend of mine who had knelt weeping with me to pray to God for life and peace.

"Some men know God in a way that I do not, though I have long thought of him. Pray to God for me, that if it be His will, I too, some day may know Him." Such movements, in the Mohammedan world, are an evidence of the unsatisfying nature of Islam as a religion.

If we go with the cross of Christ in our hearts, we shall go forth to conquer, and the crescent shall soon fade before the glory of our returning Lord. May God help us each one to feel the responsibility for those who are dying with no hope in Jesus.

After the death of Mohammed, the succession was disputed, although the Sheahs affirm that Mohammed had already designated Ali as his successor. The succession appeared to belong by right, as well as by nature, to Ali, who was married to Fatimeh, the only surviving daughter of the prophet. But it was not until the accession and assassination of Abu Bekr, Omar and Othman, that the magnanimous Ali was elected to the caliphate. Even then, he was not permitted to enjoy the long-deferred honors without an opposition which eventually proved fatal, not only to himself but also the continuation of the caliphate in the family of the founder of the faith. When Ali was in turn assassinated, his oldest son, Hassan, assumed the caliphate, to which he was peacefully elected by the people of Medina or Medineh. At the head of a powerful army, he marched to encounter Noaviyeh. The enthusiasm of his generals and forces promised a decisive victory, but Hassan was a man of peaceable disposition, averse to active life, and prefering the tranquil domesticity of a private citizen. He proposed to abdicate in favor of Noaviyeh, reserving the succession to himself after the death of Noaviyeh, who was much the elder, and an ample revenue during a life of ease and retirement at Medina. The terms of the pacification were accepted and religiously followed by Noaviyeh. Yezeed, his son, foreseeing that the approaching death of his father would restore the virtuous Hassan to the caliphate, caused the latter to be poisoned by one of his wives.

Hussein, a brother of Hassan, was a man of different metal. He had opposed his brother's abdication, and he now perceived, after escaping a plot to assassinate him, that the empire was not large enough to contain himself and Yezeed in peace. He, therefore, boldly prepared for a final conflict that was to decide the claims of the Aliites and the Ommiades. Escaping from Medina, whose governor had schemed to entrap him, Hussein hastened with his family to Kufa. The inhabitants of Kufa had hardly sent a pressing message to Hussein to resort to their city, with the offer of a powerful host, and their homage, when they allowed themselves to be easily diverted from their purpose by the swift messenger sent by Yezeed, who was ordered to seize Kufa.

But, Hussein was a man of courage, and, what was more, a true believer in predestination. "What is written, is written," is the doctrine of the Koran, of what worth is faith, if it will not bear the test in the hour of trial? What better occasion could offer for the son of Ali to testify to his descent from the prophet, and to his unflinching belief in the tremendous *fiat of Kismet*. Therefore, accompanied by his family and a score or two of Arab horsemen, Hussein went forth unflinchingly to meet his doom. The heroism of Hussein was the more remarkable, because from the outset of his journey he was oppressed by a presentment of death stalking in his path across the desert, and rapidly overtaking the small troop of devoted victims wearily marching to the grave. "To God we belong, and to God we return," was his utterance. His four brothers, sons of Ali by another wife, and all his companions also declined to accept the safe conduct offered to them, choosing to share the fate Hussein. In the meantime, the enemy's forces had planted themselves between the camp of Hussein and the Euphrates, and to the other horrors of this terrible hour was now added that of thirst, in a land quivering with intolerable heat.

The last night in the little camp was one of solemn preparation, of portentous dreams and fateful gloom. Zeineb and Hussein, brother and sister, the children of

Ali and Fatimeh, held mournful converse on the creeping horrors of the morrow, the day that should see the destruction of the family of the prophet of God. Around them gathered, one by one, their children and kinfolks and the small band of faithful defenders. Hussein urged them to fly while yet there was time, for the enemy sought only the life of one, his own. "Allah forbid that we desert you now," exclaimed Abbass, and all united in exclaiming with him that they would die with Hussein. The time for deliberation was past; there remained for them but one thing—to die. The attack was begun by Shemr, a fierce partisan. The combat continued until the hour for noon prayer, when there came a cessation of arms. During the truce Hussein chanted the "Song of Fear." Hussein fell pierced with over thirty wounds, and his head was struck off by the ferocious Shemr, who carried it all gory to Obeid Allah. Among the slain were eighteen descendants of Ali and Fatimeh. Zeineb and some of the women were spared, and eventually taken into the presence of Yezeed, together with the heads of Hussein and his brothers. Yezeed acted with moderation, and the remaining descendants of the prophet seemed to have retired from further participation in public affairs, laying aside ambition and merging themselves into the life of private citizens or of religious teachers and expounders of the faith.

Assuming the office of vindicator of the growing sect of Sheahs, who cherished the memory of Ali, Al Muchtar entered on a mission of extermination against all who were concerned in the slaughter of Hussein. The entire Mohammedan world from Afghanistan to the Straits of Gibralter now seemed to acknowledge the sway of the caliphs of the line of Moaviyeh and his successors. The rival claims of Ali and his family appeared laid at rest and forgotten. But no; in Iran, or Persia, the sectaries of Ali were slowly biding their time. It is not a little singular that not at Mecca nor at Medina, where the prophet first proclaimed his doctrines, were the claims of his children accepted, but in a distant land peopled by another race. His children were buried in foreign soil, and the honor accorded to their memory is to be found not in Arabia, but in Persia. This may be due in part to the fact that one of the wives of Hassan was a daughter of Yezdigerd, the last monarch of the Sassanian line. Her remains were brought to her native land, and her tomb is shown on the rocky heights which overlook the extensive ruins of Rhei, the last capital of the Sassanides, where she bade her father farewell.

Moslems of Persia say that when Hussein was to be beheaded, he was very thirsty, and asked for a drink of water before being beheaded. But this request was not granted and he was executed with his thirst unquenched. In memory of this tragedy there may now be seen walking the streets of Persian cities every warm summer day men carrying a bottle or jar of water and crying. "Sakkaw, sakkaw," (their name) and giving water to any who may be thirsty in the name of Hussein. Moslems take this drink in a cup carried by the sakkaw, but a Christian must furnish his own cup or drink from the palms of his hands. If offered one or two cents the sakkaw will take it, but he never asks for money. The killing of Hussein and his followers occurred in the month called Mooharram. This entire month is observed as a time of lamentation for Hassan. Hussein and their followers who were slain. During this period every man, woman and child of the Shute Moslems are under obligations to wear black garments. The last ten days of Mooharram are observed in a fanatical spirit as a revival of religion. This period is called Ashara, meaning ten days. The first seven days are for prepar-

ation. The mosque will be crowded with men and
women. The Masya-Kahns, or revivalist priests, are in
charge of these services. Followed by a large procession this priest goes to the mosque and mounting a high
pulpit preaches to large crowds. His general theme is
tragic tales, stories of martyrs, the manner of their
death, their last utterances, and the wailing and moan-
of their friends and relatives. Often in the concluding
words of a pathetic story, the entire audience, sometimes
numbering thousands, will be deeply moved and slapping
their foreheads with the palms of their hands will cry
aloud to give vent to their emotion. The mosques cannot accommodate all the worshipers during this period,
so some parts of a street are laid with carpets and rugs
where the people sit while listening to preaching. The
last three days are the most solemn. These people form
different companies, and each company visits from one
mosque to another. Passing through the streets the
men bearing the national and religious emblems are
followed by musicians playing mournful dirges with
such instruments as drum, flute and cymbal. Surrounding the musicians are hundreds of men marching with
bare breasts, shouting "Hassan, Hussein! Hassan, Hussein!" and pounding upon their breasts with bare
hands. Following them is another band surrounding a Say-yid a descendant of Ali and all of them are
shouting "Hassan, Hussein" and beating their breasts.
Next in the procession comes a band of ascetic Dervishes, wearing neither hat nor shoes nor other garments than a pair of pants, when the weather is mild.
Holding in their hands a whip about two feet long and
one or two inches in diameter made of small iron
strands, they beat their bare shoulders and back with
the same as they march shouting "Yahu, Yamal-hu,"
which are names of their god. Following comes
another band of Dervishes bearing in one hand a

knotty club to which is fastened nails, bits of brass, etc. With the other hand they beat their breasts as they repeat the cry of the preceding band. These worshipers torture the flesh by beating it thus and bruise it black.

The greatest demonstration of all occurs on the last of the ten days at sunrise, the crowds of former days gather around the mosques to start again on the marches. On this day there are also fresh recruits. In front of the mosque is a band of fifty to one hundred men and boys of 13 to 40 years of age. They are barefooted, and uniformed with a white shirt over the other clothing that reaches to the feet. Held in the right hand before each one is a two-edged sword. The left hand rests on the belt of the soldier next in front. The leader standing at the head of the band recites their creed: "Allah is God and the only God, Mohammed is the prophet of God and Ali is his vicar." All the band repeat this creed. Immediately the leader smites his own brow with his sword and this act is immitated by all his followers. Soon the faces and white clothing of the men are red with blood. Bleeding they go marching through the streets shouting: "Hassan Hussein," and waving their swords in harmony with step and voice. Fearing that these zealous young men may lose all regards for life, and inflict upon themselves mortal blows, relatives or friends frequently walk near with long sticks in hand to hinder them from such deeds. This band first marches to the court-house to be seen by the governor. Every band has the right to ask the governor for the freedom of some one prisoner, and these requests are always granted, no matter what the crime of the imprisoned. These bleeding men are as martyrs, and would go direct to heaven if death resulted from these self-inflicted wounds. After the parade ends the bloody shirts of these men are divided among their friends and kept as holy relics. The men who compose these bands are usually the most wicked in the community. They go through these ceremonies for the remission of sins and to redeem themselves in the eyes of others; but they usually continue in their wickedness as time goes on.

Another important feature of the last day in the procession is a richly decorated hearse containing a coffin, in which lies a man representing the corpse of Hassan. Beside the coffin sits a woman, the widow of Hassan, dressed in sackcloth and her head covered with dust. Following the hearse are three beautiful Arabian horses, finely saddled and harnessed, with a flake of gold, embedded with pearls, on their foreheads. On two of them are seated two girls, representing the daughters of martyrs. The tops of the girls' heads are covered with dust and straw. The third horse is riderless, to remind one of the missing martyr. Following next, is a large number of women, boys and girls, and some men —all with yokes about their necks, their hands chained behind them, seated on horses and mules. These are to represent the captives taken by Yezeed, the captain who killed Hussein. Near them are men in helmets, to represent the soldiers of Yezeed. They are armed with whips, and are driving these women and children of Moslems into captivity. Next in line, may be seen false heads raised aloft on poles, representing Yezeed, Mawya and other ancient enemies of Hussein. Boys and men gather around them, spitting at and reviling them.

Gathered, all the sword bearers, chain strikers, and the many men beating their breasts, make a great crowd and tremendous noise. The bystander is struck with horror when two fanatical bands meet, each trying to excel the other in self-mutilation. Then are frightful gashes cut; the thumping of chains on bruised bodies and the pounding of breasts is heard louder than before. With an upward sweep of the right arm, every man cries in a loud voice, "Ya Ali, Ya Ali!" as the companies pass each other.

At 4 p. m. on the last day, the marching ceases and the throng halts by some tents pitched in the middle of a public square. The swords and chain strikers approach the tents, and with a shout of victory utter the names of Ali, Hassan and Hussein, then set fire to the tents and burn them and their contents to the ground. They imagine that their enemies were in those tents, and now that they have been destroyed it is a time of great rejoicing. The marching clubs disband and the active ones are soon found at the mosques, drinking sherbet, a sweet drink, as a sort of reward for performing their religious duties.

The last night is called watch-night, and many Moslems do not even slumber during the night. It is a holy night, in which Hussein and other martyrs were buried in the tombs. It is a dishonor, and even a sin, for them to go to bed without meditation on their prophets. In the mosque services the people shout, "Oh, Hassan and Hussein, let my soul be a sacrifice for thee." They believe the observance of that night is absolute remission of sins; that the gates of heaven are open to all believers, for the sake of martyrs. Some pious Moslems preserve the tears of that night in small bottles, as it is believed they will cure disease when applied to the brows of sick men. These tears are prized as a most holy relic. The Mussulmen say: "Even David, the prophet, believed in the efficacy of tears when he wrote in the Psalms, 'Put Thou my tears in Thy bottle, oh, God.'"

On the last night many Shute Moslems walk to the mosque in bare feet wearing sack cloth. Often a governor or lord accompanied by forty to one hundred servants, all barefooted, will be seen slowly trending their way toward a mosque. At daybreak these solemn ceremonies end. Thus thousands of people every year, in different parts of the country, will slash their bodies to pieces and suffer death, believing this the way of obtaining salvation.

Mohammedan followers are not to salute those who drink, nor to marry those who are intemperate, nor to sit at the table where there is wine. Some one asked Ali how strict they should be regarding strong drink. Ali answered that if one drop of wine should fall in a well and the well should be filled up with earth and after a hundred years had passed away a sheep should eat grass growing on that spot, he, Ali, would not eat of that flock. Again, Ali, the son-in-law and cousin of Mohammed, said that if there was a caravan of camels reaching from the north pole to the south pole and the last camel in the caravan should have wine on his back, that he, Ali, would not take hold of the bit of the head camel. Mohammed said that in hell there is a valley in which there burn 1,000 loads of wood every day; there is a house in that valley and in that house a box, and in that box there is a fiery snake which has 100 heads and every head has 100 mouths and every mouth has 100 teeth and every tooth has 100 stingers and every stinger has 100 poisons. The people asked Mohammed: " Who will be punished there?" and he answered: " Those who are intemperate." They classed the Jews as an inferior people, yet Mohammed said that it was easier for a Jew to enter Heaven than for a person who drank wine. If a person drinks wine at night, God will look upon him with his bad eye* until morning; also his prayer will not be heard for forty days and forty nights. But lately the opium has been introduced in all parts of Persia, whereas

*The Mohammedans believe that God has two eyes, one good the other evil, that with the good eye he watches over the Mahammedans, with the evil eye over the Christian and all non Mohammedans.

the Mohammedans are becoming more and more slaves of it.

Some regard Ali, Hassan and Hussein as first of all creatures, the supreme intercessors, and endowed with divine light. Ali is the greatest of all. On him rests the hope of salvation. The Moslem believes in written prayers and passages or verses from the Koran. These are laid on a cloth and placed in leather cases, and are seen suspended from the neck or tied to the arm for protection.

Charms with the names of the Imams engraved on the stones and beads from Kerballa are carried with them as the belief is that these keep a man from accident, evil eye and robbery.

The Mohammedans when they cut their finger nails wrap them in paper or in cloth and throw them behind their heads. Their idea is that God will ask where their finger nails are, and they will say that they have them on their back. Others will save them and bury them with the person at his death.

If a man has two wives and loves one more than the other, the one that has been slighted will go to the Persian priest and tell him the case, then he will send her to her husband to bring one hair out of his head, also one of her own. When she returns with these the priest will read a few verses out of the Holy Koran, and then take the two hairs, burn them, and put the ashes in a glass of water, which the woman must give to her husband, who will thenceforth love her more than the other one, as the power of the words of the prophet having been read over the glass of water. it will lead him to love her.

All the Mohammedans believe that Mohammed stands at the gate of heaven. They believe that when they go to heaven he will let them pass safely over the bridge, which is sharper than any two-edged sword and thin as a hair. When a person of some other religion comes, he will slacken the hair and then the person will be cast into hell. They feel that they are contaminated by touching the Christian Bible, and great care is exercised to keep the Koran out of the hands of the Christians.

Jonah was three days and nights in the belly of a whale. After this example, some Persians fast three days and three nights; after that they bring seven kinds of grains, and mixing them together, add seven parts of salt and eat it: then they retire and dream that they are very thirsty, and that some one of the opposite sex is giving them water—and then that person will be their mate.

Once a camel strayed into a mosque, mistaking it for a caravansary. All the worshipers got around it, declaring that even the dumb beast recognizes the presence of the prophet. They decorated and arrayed it and then paraded through the streets, each one taking some of the hairs of the animal as a blessing, and the animal became an attache of the mosque.

The blessings of medicine are unknown in Persia, with the exception of several medical missionaries. The Persian doctors have not become such by studying books on medical science, however there are many quack doctors who have a system of superstition which has been taught them orally by older men. Blades of some kinds of grasses which are known to medical science as having no medicinal properties are the chief remedies prescribed for disease. Internal diseases are called supernatural and it is believed they are inflicted by evil spirits. None of the doctors can do anything for these forms of diseases, as they consider it out of their realm. A patient with an internal disease is sent to the priest who will diagnose the case by looking into the Koran or some other superstitious books in which he

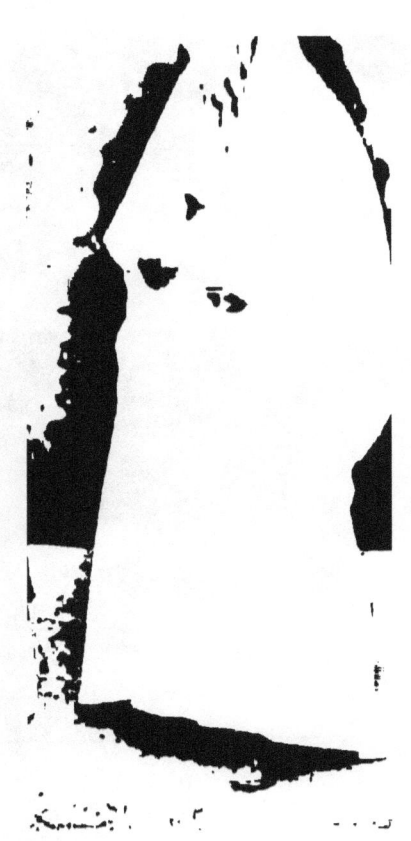

CHURNING.   Page 134.
GRINDING WHEAT.   Page 132.

locates the particular demon that is afflicting the patient. He will write some mystical signs on two slips of paper, the priest gives direction for their use, (this one soak in a cup of water, the other bind on the patient's arm). There are several remedies for fever, one is to tie seven knots in a white thread and fasten it around the waist, wearing it fifteen or twenty days, they believe this will cure the fever. Another remedy is to remove the clothing and jump into cold water before breakfast. If a man has a severe attack of colic and cries "I die, I die," his friends run for the nearest baldheaded man, as he is known to have power to remove the pains by firmly pressing the smooth surface of his cranium against the surface of the patient's body nearest the seat of pain. Pork is never used as food, but it is believed to remove rheumatism when bound on the parts affected.

There are two great needs in Persia at present native preachers and native doctors. May the dear Lord help us to hope and pray that the Mohammedan Dominion may in God's own time be brought down, this dark spot in the civilization of this closing nineteenth century be blotted out, and the way be opened up for the Gospel to be preached, received and professed freely by the followers of the false prophet in every land where they exist. If the power of the Sultan and Shah were destroyed, the downfall of Mohammedism before the Gospel would probably follow speedily, the crescent would wane and disappear, while the cross would shine resplendently in its stead.

HISTORICAL MISSION WORK.

Religiously Persia is a very important link in the chain of Moslem lands from Morocco to the walls of China and the frontiers of India. This chain we may consider as broken in a measure by the French occupation of Algiers and the British occupation of Egypt and Russia's annexation of the great khanates of Turkestan. Of the four independent Moslem powers, Morocco, Turkey. Persia and Afghanistan. Persia has probably the most innate vitality and the best prospect of national life, and is at the same time the most open to religious change. In Turkey the Sultan is caliph, the government is a theocracy, and the teachers of religion must be kept in harmony with the state. In Persia there is more antagonism. The king and his rulers are glad to humble the Mollahs and not infrequently the highest Mushtahid of a city is called to the capitol or cast into prison because he has overstepped his limit and excited mobs or riot or opposed the civil governor. In this conflict between the civil and eccliastical powers there is an opening for a large degree of toleration. Large communities of people in Persia were never content under the Moslem system and they wear it as a yoke. The Ali Illahees form the majority of the population in some districts, and in other districts the Babis, adherents of a mystical belief that is undermining the whole structure of Islam.

Persia is not yet like Japan, a nation in search of a religion, but there are many indications that the cycle of Islam is drawing to a close, and thousands are weary and heavy laden, and some are hearing the voice of Jesus say, "Come unto me, and I will give you rest."

In Kurdistan and some parts of Persia live the Yezidees or Devil-Worshipers. Hundreds of them have been killed in the attempt to force them under the yoke of Islam. These poor heathenish people in their distress turn to missionaries and beg to be enrolled as Protestants and to receive Christian instruction. They are verily a heathen race with Satan enthroned as their chief deity. Their belief is that for 10,000 years the government of this world is committed by the Supreme

God to His Satanic Majesty. Among the Jews, who number about 50,000 in these parts of Persia and Kurdistan mountains, there is a similar unrest. Some are looking to Jerusalem for orders to return. Some are asking when will our Messiah come, and some are reading the evidence and saying, "He has come." Some also who at first are drawn by the words of Jesus fall back into the subtle pantheistic doctrines of Babism. It is a singular fact that in Russia some of the dissenters from the established Church have embraced Judaism, and quite as singular that in Persia there is a tendency of dissenting Jews to accept Babism. But here again, there is the better sign that Jesus Christ by His character and His cross and His Spirit from on high, is in the hearts of this long exiled people.

The field of Persia contains a large number of nominal Christians as well as Jews. The heart of Kurdistan is in that field and we are called upon to have a great share. O, how little is done for great Kurdistan, whose people number about 5,000,000. Taken together what a marvelous field it is! What field anywhere can compare with it for marvelous variety and wonderful possibility? We are laying foundations and can see but little, but the great Master Builder is going to rear a temple there. What a temple it will be when all the varied stones have been quarried and polished and built onto Christ the corner-stone? Three great racial families of the globe, Aryan, Semitic and Turanian, are here represented. The contrasts in natural scenery are no more striking than those of races. The snowy crags of Jelu, the burning plains of Mesopotamia, the rocky canyons of Ravandooz, the deep gorges of the Zab, the fertile plains of Oroomiah are no more dissimilar than are the Armenian, the suave Jacobite, the crafty Persian, the stolid Turk, the wild Arab, the savage Kurd, the patient Jew, and the oppressed Nestorian.

There is the orthodox Islam of the Sunni, the heretical Islam of the Shiah, the reformed Islam of the Babi, and the heathenish Islam of the Ali-Illahi. Again, since Persia became Mohammedan and so far closed to Christian truth, God has opened special ways of access to the people. His providence has in the turmoil of the centuries, planted here and there through the land, fragments of Christian churches. To relight in these the candle of the spirits presence, long since extinct, has been an essential step toward illuminating the surrounding mass of Mohammedan darkness.

History began in Persia. Eden was in or within her borders. The builders of Babel had come "from the east" to the land of two rivers. There was the home of civilization and the nursery of the nations. Iran or Persia in its largest sense was a true center of population, of knowledge, of languages and of arts, which instead of traveling westward only, as has been fancifully supposed, or eastward as might with equal reason have been asserted were expanded in all directions, to all regions of the world. Of the founder of the Persian Empire, Isaiah prophecied, "thus saith the Lord to His annointed, to Cyrus, whose right hand I have holden to subdue nations before him." I will go before thee. Cyrus is my shepherd, and will perform all my pleasure. Thus, by the hand of God, the little kingdom of Pars on the gulf, Iran, widened and conquered till it comprised the western half of Asia, and the lower valley of the Nile. The great empire to some degree symbolized the glorious and everlasting kingdom of Jesus Christ, and Cyrus was a type of the great shepherd of the sheep. By Cyrus and his successors the Jews were delivered from the Assyrians, were restored to Judea with their consecrated vessels of silver and gold, and were authorized and protected in rebuilding Jerusalem. A large part of the race, however, remained in the land of captivity and were saved from destruction by the beautiful queen Esther; they had dispersed to all the hundred and twenty-seven provinces of Xerxes, and the dominion of Cyrus had included also the cities of the Medes to which the ten tribes had been carried away. It is worthy of note also, that the Persians were the one people who could sympathize with the Jews in the hatred of idolatry, and there is evidence that a Persian version of the Old Testament was used in the synagogues. From this data, notwithstanding the fact that the chosen people were exiled for their disloyalty to Jehovah, we may safely infer that his word and worship were carried throughout the vast empire of their captors in Persia as in the Roman Empire, the dispersion was a Providential preparation for Christianity.

Persia's historic relation to the kingdom of God began, it may be, when the wise men from the East seeing his star came and worshiped the new born King; they were Persians, as their coming forshadowed the bowing of Persia and all nations to our Lord; and when the fulfilment of the prophecy "I will pour out my spirit on all flesh," began at Pentecost, the strangers present whose names are first on the list are "Parthians, Medes, Elamates," all dwellers in this same land. Peter himself, accompanied by his wife, toiled over the fiery deserts, and preached at least at Babylon. Mark was with him and tradition says that two others of the apostles, also Thomas and Matthew labored in the Persian field.

Of early Persian Christianity, little is known. Historians tell us that it flourished and spread, and from the silence of history it is thought that under the Parthians there was no long and fierce persecution. But with the rise of the Persian dynasty of the Sassanides (A. D. 226), there came a revival of the ancient worship, and a determined effort was made to put down all other religion. From the time of King Sapor, when Christianity conquered heathenism in the Roman empire, the Christians of Persia threw in their sympathies with the Christian state. Almost simultaneously, therefore, with the war against Constantine, there began in the year 339 a rigorous persecution of the Christians. It continued forty years, and according to Mares, bishop of Seleucia at the time, furnished 160,000 martyrs. This may be an exaggeration, but the Syrian "Acts of Persian Martyrs" records their great numbers and terrible sufferings. In 410, the tolerant Zazdgird I. permitted a synod of Christians to meet in his capital, and sent the primate of the church on a mission to the Roman Emperor. The severe persecutions of his successor, Bahman V., a favorite hero of Persian tradition, ended with the war with Rome in 422. Religious freedom was then guaranteed by treaty to Zoroastrians in the Roman empire, and to Christians in Persia. But the accession of his son, Yazdegird II., in 438, was marked by renewed persecution of Jews and Christians. In consequence, a rebellion in Armenia was not quelled until the king promised to his subjects complete liberty of worship. Those were also times of fearless missionary enterprise. In 334, a bishop was settled in far-off Tros, in Khorassan. A metropolitan, implying several bishops and numerous converts, existed in Mero as early as 420 A. D., and about that time a see was established at Herat.

During these centuries the mind of Persia was thoroughly hostile to the kingdom of Jesus Christ. Her philosophy and religion furnished the germs of many of the great heresies—Gnosticism, Manichaeism, and other systems of theosopy, that rent the Christian church. Bishop Nestorius, of Constantinople, was willing to call Mary the Mother of God, but denied her divinity, and he held to the union of two natures in one person in Christ. Falsely accused, he was condemned unheard, and banished. His followers, finally driven from the Roman Empire in 489 A. D., found a home in Persia. Borsumos, the founder of the seminary at Nisibis, which sent out so many learned missionaries, had worked for his fellow believers from 440 to 485, with such marvelous enterprise and skill that they became the chief Christian sect of the country.

It was the mission of the Nestorians to carry the Gospel to the great heathen East, and they were not unfaithful to their opportunity. "For centuries," says Tracy in his history, "they maintained missions in Tartary, China and other eastern regions." Their churches were scattered from Syria and Cyprus to Pekin, and from the coasts of Malabar and Ceylon to the borders of Siberia. Some of the Chinese emperors favored Christianity, and ordered the erection of numerous churches. The converts are supposed to have numbered more than the Greek and Latin communions. If the monument of Sigan Fu, China, is trustworthy, they had preached Christ in that land before 636 A. D. Prominent mention should be made here of the scholar and missionary, Subchalyesu, who about the close of the eighth century, preached with great success to the Gelae on the Caspian shore. Though formal compacts of toleration may not have been made by Mahammed and Omar with the Nestorians, as has been asserted by some writers and denied by others, yet many of them occupied high places of state during the Arabic domination. And though the Arabs ruled the country from the decisive battle of Nehorvend, in 462, yet Islam was compelled to compromise with the more flexible and more tolerant genius of the Persians. Hence the churches' opportunities for proselytism. But with all its opportunities and achievements, Nestorianism never rose to be more than a sect of Christianity, in which "the simplicity of the gospel was fashioned and painted with the colors of the Syriac theology." Its power was vitiated by superstition and therefore it proved unable to permanently mould and purify the nations. By the year 1000 Islam was advancing and by the year 1300 had gained the ascendency in the countries east of the Caspian, where Christianity had long been firmly established. The bigoted and zealous Mohammed, sultan of Cabul in the eleventh century, had, it is thought, made millions of Moslems by his sword. And when, at the end of the fourteenth century, the ferocious Tamerlane, the greatest of conquerors, swept over Asia like a whirlwind of fire, there followed the terrible anarchy and persecution that shrivelled and blasted the churches. Romish missions also accelerated their rapid decline. By 1500 A. D. Nestorian Christianity was almost extinct in the lands of its greatest triumphs. The miserable remnant of the church, that for five centuries had carried the cross over Asia, was discovered early in the present century hid away in the mountains of Kurdistan.

John de Monte Corvino, the great Romish missionary to the Mongols and Chinese and who became archbishop of Pekin, labored at Tabriz, Persia, near the end of the thirteenth century. His work was short, but very successful. Speedy conversions, however, were followed by speedy defections. About 1341 A. D. the Romanists produced a faulty and interpolated translation of the four Gospels. In the seventeenth century they seemed to have, at least, a firm foothold in the country, but their influence gradually weakened. Now they have missions in several cities with schools, churches and two or three small nunneries; all the work of the present century. The number of the pupils and converts is about 5,000.

In 1747, two heroic Moravians, Hocker and Rueffer, medical missionaries, penetrated to Ispahan to work among the fire-worshipers. They suffered repeated robbery and hardship such as being compelled to travel over the deserts in the burning sun on foot and nearly naked. Because of the anarchy and misery of the land under Nadir Shah, they left the country, unable to accomplish anything. With the nineteenth century dawned the ora of evangelical missions in Persia. Among the worthy men devoted to this work was Henry Martyn. On June 9, 1811, he reached Shiraz from India. In that city of Persian learning and Moslem bigotry, "seat of satan," as he named it, he revised his translation of the New Testament, and boldly preached the Son of God. The story of that work, his controversies with the keenest teachers of Islam, of his terrible journey to present a copy of the translation to the Shah, his three months' sickness at Tabriz, his last ride, and lonely death at Tocat, October 16, 1812, has inspired his successors for more than 80 years. (No finer missionary consecration has blessed the Church of Christ.)

In 1829, Rev. Dr. Pfander, of the Basle society, entered Tabriz. The fruit of his brief labor was various treatises, and in particular the important "Balance of Truth," exhibiting the evidences of Mohammedanism and Christianity. Rev. Frederick Hans and other Germans after a four-years' struggle with unscrupulous bigotry at Tabriz, were compelled to withdraw in 1837. Grover worked at Bagdad from 1829 to 1833, and Merrick in various parts of the country, from 1835 to 1845. Their efforts, largely failures, were mainly on behalf of Mussulmans. Dr. William Glen, of the Scottish Missionary Society, entered the field in July, 1838. He had spent several years at Astrachan, Russia, where he had worked at a Persian translation of the Old Testament. Completing this in 1847, he went to Scotland to superintend the printing. At the age of 70 he returned, and lived at Teheran, to aid in circulating the Scriptures. In the court of the old Armenian church in that city, is a *mural* tablet in his memory. What stars will shine in their crowns, who opened to Persia's millions the word of life. About 1832, Messrs. Smith and Dwight were sent by the A. B. C. F. M. to explore the regions of Northern Persia. They decided to establish a mission among the Nestorians.

In 1835 Messrs. Perkins and Grant were appointed the first missionaries; they arrived at Oroomiah and established a school. The school room was in a basement. They had no books, but just used wall cards. The studies were confined to the Bible, a little arithmetic and geography. The pupils consisted of bishops, priests, elders and deacons of the old Nestorian Church. In 1843 Mr. Stoddard was appointed superintendent of the school in "Sery," about three miles from Oroomiah city. The condition of women in Persia in the year 1835 when the missionaries first went there was very different from that of today. At that time only one woman in the whole country could read. Her name was Helena, the sister of the Patriarch. At that time the houses were large, and the whole family connection lived in the one home, sometimes thirty in one house. Women were treated as slaves. After doing the housework they had to work in the fields like men and care for their little ones while they worked. At the same time they were often brutally abused by their husbands and called cats, cows, donkeys, etc. The first missionaries were greatly used by God to scatter the deep darkness. It was with great difficulty that they found opportunity to teach a few small girls a short time each day. The work progressed very slowly. In 1843 the well known Miss Fisk established a boarding school. She only understood one word in the Syriac language, the word "girl." When she would meet with the people, she would ask for a girl and pass on. The people thought that she wanted to make bees of them and make them fly to America, so they would not let them go. At last she found four, and one morning while sitting in her room she saw Mar Yohannan coming with two girls. She met him at the door, and her heart was so full of love that she wept for joy. He told her that they were her property and none could take them away. She had no books. The lessons were written on a long paper and hung on the walls. Out of these schools hundreds of young men and women have been educated and enlightened and fed on the living word of God, and they have indeed been as salt to every house or community they have gone to.

All the work of the American board in Persia was in 1871 transferred to the Presbyterian board of the United States of America. At present they have about twenty-four hundred communicants and large attendance in their schools. In 1869 the English Missionary Society occupied Ispahan later on also Bushire. American missionaries are at present located at Teheran, Hamadan, Tabriz and Oroomiah. A number of out-stations are occupied by native helpers and the rest of the ten millions are practically uncared for. A majority of the large cities and nearly all of the smaller ones are not even occupied as out-stations. In 1887 Arch-bishop of Canterbury, London, sent missionaries to Oroomiah who are co-operating with the Nestorian Church. In 1894 the Lutheran missionaries for Mohammedans, under the auspices of Pastor Faber of Berlin, Germany, were sent to make their headquarters at Oroomiah. The missionaries were Zerweek and Kitzle ; but they were not careful enough to conceal their plan of labor and told everywhere their intentions and desires for the future. The plan was made public by the press as well as by words. All their plans were communicated to the Shah of Persia, who telegraphed his order to these missionaries to leave at once his country and depart from its borders. As there is no religious liberty among the Mohammedan public as yet, all applications were in vain, and the saddest thing in the whole trouble was the early and unexpected death of Pastor Kitzle, a young and learned minister of the Gospel, who found his grave in a country where he was not allowed to live and labor for Christ and the salvation of souls. His companion, Dr. Zerweek, returned to Germany.

There is another grand work which needs our attention, the work which has been accomplished by Pastor Peria Yohannan, a native of Persia and a graduate of Hermansburg, Germany, and who received his support from there. The pastor's work has been largely in Wazeriwa and the neighboring villages. Much has been done by his effort in teaching, preaching and spreading God's word. The simplicity of his living and the manner of conducting his work has much to do with his success.

THE KURDS.

Kurdistan is a geographical name applied to the Kurdistan Mountains, and sometimes to the whole country inhabited by the Kurds. The area is estimated at 50,000 square miles, extending to Mt. Ararat, in Armenia, on the north, to the plains of the Tigris on the south, to the city of Harput, Sivan, on the west, and to the plains of Oroomiah and the city of Sakis on the east. Thus, this territory is partly subject to the Shah of Persia and partly to the Sultan of Turkey. The boundary line is a point of dispute, although in A. D. 1639 a treaty between the Shah Sefavi and one of the Sultans of Turkey established the frontier line, which since has served as a nominal line between the two empires. On the territory here described not only Kurds reside, but also Turks, Armenians, Chaldeans, Assyrians and Persians. The Kurds are descendants of the ancient Carduchi, with whom Xenophon and the 10,000 had so long a struggle. The region they occupy is as rugged as their character. They are by far the most turbulent of the subjects of the Shah, and were it not for the beautiful rugs they manufacture in their rude dwellings, one would be at a loss to imagine a reason for their existence. Their origin is wrapt in obscurity; they seem to have no relationship with any other race, and as with Cain, their hand is against everyone and everyone's hand against them. The ethymologist who places little value on his life, might find a few months among the mountains of Kurdistan of some profit to science. They, themselves, claim that they are descendants of Esau. They speak a mixed language, collected from Persian, Syrian and Arabic languages. Their language is called Kurmanji, and has never been reduced to writing, so they are without books or schools. If any writing is done, it is done in the Persian or Arabic characters. They number about 5,000,000; 700,000 are subjects of the Shah, and a few to the Sultan of Turkey, but practically all are lawless and beyond the control of either of these two governments. A Kurd is very decided and independent in spirit. He would rather live in a cave under a projecting rock, and be unmolested, than to dwell in a palace and be subject to higher authority. Some of the tribes have a small village in the mountains, to which they return in winter. Their houses are made of stone and clay, and are usually under projecting rocks or on the slope of a hill. The roof is so low that a man cannot stand erect.

The Kurds very seldom cultivate the soil, but keep herds of cattle and horses and flocks of sheep, and travel from place to place, wherever they may find good pastures for their flock. A Kurd goes before his sheep, having a staff in his hand, and on his shoulder hangs a bag in which he has provisions for the day. He gives names to his sheep, and when he calls a certain sheep it comes to him. He often may be seen sitting, singing and playing his flute, his fond flock gathered around about him for an audience. But the principal occupation is robbery. Many may be seen asleep during the day, but they rise at sunset and start on their robbing expeditions. The Kurd has a spear in one hand, sword at his side, pistol and dagger in his belt, with many cartridges, and a gun in the other hand. Dark eyes, and a turban covering much of his forehead, makes him a fearful looking fellow. When they start at dusk they are ready to rob and kill; by the next day at 9 o'clock, they return with their prey of flocks, herds and valuable goods, and then rest for a time.

During the greater part of summer they live in tents in the cool places on the mountain slopes and in the valleys. In winter they dwell in houses built under ground most of them containing only one room, with one or two small holes on the top for light. This one apartment answers the purpose of bedroom, parlor, kitchen and stable. In daytime all inmates are out, but towards sunset they come dropping in, one by one, at least a score of them, men, women and children. The hens, however, have already turned in in advance and are perched in a corner for the night; sheep, oxen and horses have been stalled, each in its well-known place. After night has fairly set in, coarse, stale bread and sour milk are brought in for supper. Two spoons and one big dish is all the plate, and the spoons are passed to each in turn— all in the dark, as they have no lights. It is now bedtime, and one after the other finds his place under the same quilt, without a pillow or bed, except perhaps some hay spread on the floor. In a few minutes all are fast asleep, and soon the heavy breathing and snoring of men and cattle is mingled, and the effect is anything but pleasant to the ear.

Parents teach their children how to become successful

thieves. A father will give his son of 6 or 7 years of age, a pistol, dagger and shield and then play robber with the child, showing him how to use these deadly instruments. A Kurd once told the writer of his timid son. The child was afraid to steal. The father wanted to make him a successful thief and so tried the following plan: The first night he sent the child to steal grapes from his own yard; the second night corn from his own crib; the third night grapes from a stranger, next a chicken, then a sheep, then to enter a house, and so on until the youth became a most daring highway robber. Then the father was proud of his son and told him that he had become a man and could marry. The girls of these tribes will not marry a man until his reputation as a successful robber is established. They wish to be assured that they will not starve after marriage. The Kurds are divided into tribes, each tribe having a chief. These tribes are generally enemies with one another. The chief of a tribe will lead his men against another tribe and kill all the men and take the flocks, herds and all other property as booty. But they do not harm the women and children. An old man is not honored by a tribe. They say he can't fight nor rob and is good for nothing but to feed sheep. The man most highly honored is the one who has killed the most men. When a man is killed in battle, or while robbing, he is honored at the funeral by the singing of many songs, by weeping and lamentations, but not many tears are shed when one dies a natural death. The Kurds are very quick-tempered. A slight offense will make them enemies and they will at once seek revenge. They are very fond of fighting and war, very active and nimble in climbing mountains and in a running fight. They love to revile an enemy, and are continually trying to invent new and more severe expressions of hatred. It is their nature to quarrel and fight.

Brothers often become angered over a small matter and fight to the death. They think no more of killing a man than we do of killing a chicken. They are very licentious, especially those living in towns and cities. Husband and wife are not loyal to each other and this is frequently the cause of murder. As a people they have no foresight, having no thought for the morrow.

The Kurdish religion is Islam and that of the Sunni sect. They are very religious, pray five times a day, always before leaving their homes so as to have success in their robbery. Before each prayer they perform the ablutions; when a man is praying no woman must touch him lest she might get the benefit of his prayer, as women have no soul and if she touch him she would get his soul and he would lose it. If a woman should come near to him during his prayer the man would stop, step out of the circle of prayer and then take up his gun and shoot the woman, then continue his prayer. Their women wear an exceedingly picturesque costume. They have dark complexions, with eyes and hair intensely black. Their beauty is not of a refined type but by a mass of paint is made sufficiently attractive for their easily-pleased husbands. Almost all the work, in and out of doors, is done by them. Early in the morning when they are through with their home work they hasten to field to attend to the flocks or gather fuel for use in winter. In the evening they come in with large burdens on their backs, which appear to be quite enough for two donkeys to carry. So industrious are they that they frequently spin on their way to and from work, singing all the while apparently as happy as if all the world were theirs. The difficulties and ailments of womanhood are nothing to them. A woman with child will go out among the rocks, climbing the mountain heights. Her time of labor is at hand, but she does not cease her usual toil. In the evening a woman may be

PERSIAN BARBER

KURDISH SHEIKS.

seen coming down the mountain singing with a heavy burden of fuel on her back, and in her arms the child to which she has given birth during the day. Even this the men do not appreciate or reward, they will not hesitate, when it is raining, to drag the women from the tent to make room for a favorite steed.

Their chief priests are called Sheikhs and are honored as gods. They kneel before a chief priest and kiss his hands, clothes and shoes, and ask for his blessing. To penitent ones he promises that he will ask God to forgive their sins. He has absolute power over laymen. They believe his words as inspired truth and obey implicitly. I knew of one Sheikh who bathed every morning in a spring and the people would flock to this place to draw of the water to drink, in which he had washed his body. The father of the late Sheikh Obeidullah assisted the Sultan in the late Russian-Turkish war, commanded more than 100,000 Kurds to fight against Russia. He told them not to be afraid of the big cannons that would be seen when they met the Russians. He said, "I have by the help of Allah bound the mouth of these cannon and they cannot hurt you." It is said that he would arise every morning with black hands and claim they had been blackened by the gunpowder of these cannons, and that he had been in battle all night with the Russians and was not harmed at all. This would encourage more Kurds to go into battle, and believing this statement, they marched wildly and flew into the faces of these big guns and many thousands were slain. For a while this Sheikh had an Armenian servant, who was attending to the horse which the Sheikh himself rode, and which was one of the most excellent horses. One morning while he was taking care of the horse, he kicked him, and drawing his dagger he thrust it right through the horse; soon he was brought to answer for this and everyone was anxious to shed his blood. The servant said, "Allow me to speak a word before you take my life. How long will you be hard to believe, the horse being in the front of the battle, was struck by the enemy, but bravely defended the Sheikh." This pleased the Sheikh immensely and he gave the servant many gifts and robes, and said to the soldiers, "Look at this infidel how he has testified for me, therefore, how much more should you believe me." The servant seeing his master treat the multitude so foolishly, succeeded in treating his master in the same manner.

These wild Kurds, who are a band of robbers, have no other organization, being simply a band of robbers. Out of their number the Sultan of Turkey created the so-called Hamidieh troops in 1891. This was an application of the same principle that prompts him at other times to throw open the prison doors and invite the convicts to rob and kill Christians. These Hamidieh troops will go and attack villages, dishonor women and abduct girls of tender age. I assure you that the butchery of Sassoum was but a drop in the ocean of Christian bloodshed, occurring silently, and few by few all over the empire year after year, month after month and day after day. Innocent women and children have been shot down, clubbed to death in their houses and fields, tortured in cells, or left to exile under the scorching sun of Arabia. The piteous cry of starving children, the groans of old men who have lived to see what can never be embodied in words, the violation of maidenhood, nay of tender childhood; the shrieks of mothers made childless by crimes, compared with which murder would be a blessing; the screams of women, scarcely human, working under the lash; and all the vain voices of blood and agony that die away in that desert without having found responsive echoes—all this cannot possibly fail to find an echo in heaven sooner or later!

The founder of this religion was Zoroaster, who lived about 1200 B. C. There are two prevailing ideas about his birth-place, some believing that it was Babylonia, while others say it was Oroomiah. There are many good reasons for believing that Oroomiah was his birth-place. 1st. The original worshipers were Persians, and their religion was started in Persia ; 2d. All oriental scholars and writers suppose this was his native city ; 3d. In the district immediately surround.ng Oroomiah, there are more than twenty-five immense hills of ashes, the remaining monuments of the fire-worshipers of this region. The religious book of the Parsees is called Avesta, which means, the revelation. The language is Zend, from which the Persian language is derived.

According to Zoroaster's philosophy, our world is the work of two hostile principals—Spenta-mainyush, the good principal, and Angro-mainyush, the evil principal ; both serving under one God. All that is good in the world comes from the former ; all that is bad comes from the latter. Zoroastrian philosophy teaches that your good thoughts, good words and good deeds alone will be your intercessors. Nothing more will be wanted. They alone will save you, as a safe pilot to the harbor of Heaven, as a safe guide to the gates of Paradise. Thus, Zoroastrianism teaches the immortality of the soul. A plant called white homa, which is the emblem of immortality, is guarded by innumerable guarding spirits. The number of these guarding spirits is 99,999. Again, Zoroastrianism admits a heaven and a hell. Between heaven and this world there is supposed to be a bridge called "Genevat." According to the Parsee scriptures, for three days after a man's death his soul remains within the limits of this world, under the guidance of the angel Srosh. If the deceased be a pious man, or a man who led a virtuous life, his soul utters the words, "Well is he, by whom that, which is his benefit, becomes the benefit of anyone else." If he be a wicked man or one who led evil life, his soul utters these plaintive words: "To which land shall I turn? Whither shall I go?" On the dawn of the third night, the departed souls appear at the "Genevat bridge." This bridge is guarded by the angel Mcher Daver, i. e., Mcher, the judge. He presides there as a judge assisted by the angels Rashue and Astad, the former representing justice and the latter truth. At this bridge, and before the angel Mcher, the soul of every man has to give an account of its doings in the past life. Mcher Daver, the judge, weighs a man's actions by a scale-pan. If a man's good actions outweigh his evil ones, even by a small particle, he is allowed to pass from the bridge to the other end, to heaven; if his evil actions outweigh his good ones, even by a small weight, he is not allowed to pass over the bridge, but is hurled down into the deep abyss of hell; if his meritorious and evil deeds counter-balance each other, he is sent to a place known as "Hamast-gehan," corresponding to the Catholic "purgatory." His meritorious deeds would prevent him from going to hell, and his evil actions would not let him go to heaven. Again, Zoroastrian books say that the merit of good deeds, and the guiltiness for bad ones, increase with the growth of time, as capital increases with interest. Thus, a meritorious deed done in youth is more effective than that very deed done in advanced age.

The Parsee's places of worship are known as fire temples. They believe that the holy fire was brought down from Heaven by Zoroaster. Only high priests can approach it, and they must wear a half-mask over their face, lest their breath should defile it, and dare not ever touch it with their hands, but with golden tools.

Tobacco-smoking is prohibited, as the smoker would defile the holy fire. "In the eyes of a Parsee his holy fire's brightness, activity, purity and incorruptibility bear the most perfect semblance to the nature and perfection of the deity." In establishing a fire temple fires from various places of manufacture are brought, and kept in different vases. Great efforts are also made to obtain fire caused by lightning. Over one of these fires a perforated metallic, flat tray, with a handle attached, is held. On this tray are placed small chips and dust of fragrant sandalwood. These chips and dust are ignited by the heat of the fire below, care being taken that the perforated tray does not touch the fire. Thus a new fire is created out of the first fire. Then from this new fire another one is created by the same process. From this new fire another is again produced, and so on, until the process is repeated nine times. The fire thus prepared after the ninth process is considered pure. The fires brought from other places of manufacture are treated in a similar manner. These purified fires are all collected together upon a large vase, which is then put in its proper place in a separate chamber. Again when a Parsee goes before the sacred fire which is kept all day and night burning in the fire temples the officiating priest presents before him the ashes of a part of the consumed fire. The Parsee applies it to his forehead. A Parsee prays sixteen times during the day, the same prayers have to be repeated by the fire-worshippers. He repeats his prayers early when he arises in the morning and before and after washing, before and after each meal, etc. But three main prayers are to the sun, when the sun comes up, with bared breast he stands upon the banks of the river, as soon as the rays of the sun appear he repeats his prayer. And at noon when the sun is right above, in like manner he repeats his prayer and at night, while the sun is going down, they are all waiting to offer up their prayers to the sun which is fast disappearing. The children are always present at these prayers and are standing on the banks of the rivers and and are instructed and taught how to repeat the prayers. The following is one of the prayers to the sun or to the fire : "O, Omniscient Lord! I repent of all my sins. I repent of all evil thoughts that I might have entertained in my mind, of all the evil words that I might have spoken, of all the evil actions that I might have committed. O, Omniscient Lord! I repent of all the faults that might have originated with me, whether they refer to thoughts, words, or deeds, whether they pertain to my body or soul, whether they be in connection with the material world or spiritual."

To educate their children is a spiritual duty of Zoroastrian parents. Education is necessary, not only for the material good of the children and the parents, but also for their spiritual good. According to the Parsee books, the parents participate in the meritoriousness of the good acts performed by their children as the result of a good education, imparted to them. On the other hand, if the parents neglect the education of their children, and if as the result of this neglect, they do wonderful acts or evil deeds, the parents have a spiritual responsibility for such acts. In proportion to the malignity or evilness of these acts the parents are responsible to God for the neglect of the education of their children. It is, as it were, a spiritual self-interest that must prompt a Parsee to look to the good education of his children at an early age. The proper age recommended by religious Parsee books for ordinary education is 7. Before that age children should have home education with their parents, especially with the mother. At the age of 7, after a little religious education, a Parsee child is invested with Sudreh and Kusti, i. e., the sacred shirt and thread. A Parsee may put on the dress of any nationality he likes, but under that dress he must always wear the sacred shirt and thread. These are the symbols of his being a Zoroastrian.

These symbols are full of meaning, and act as perpetual monitors, advising the wearer to lead a life of purity, of physical and spiritual purity. A Parsee is enjoined to remove and put on again immediately the sacred thread several times during the day, saying a very short prayer during the process. He has to do so early in the morning on rising from bed, before meals and after ablutions. The putting on of symbolic thread and the accompanying short prayer remind him to be in a state of repentance for misdeeds, if any, and to preserve good thoughts, good words and good deeds.

Female education claims as much attention among the Parsees as male education. Physical education is as much spoken of in the Zoroastrian books as mental and moral education. The health of the body is considered the first requisite for the health of the soul. That the physical education of the ancient Persians, the ancestors of the modern Parsees, was a subject of admiration among the ancient Greeks and Romans is well known.

Obedience to parents is a religious virtue with the Zoroastrian religion. One of the blessings that a priest prays for in a house on performing the Afringan ceremony is the obedience of the children to the head of the family. He prays: "May obedience overcome disobedience in this house; may peace overcome dissension; may charity overcome want of charity; may courtesy overcome pride; may truth overcome falsehood." Zoroastrianism asks its disciples to keep the earth pure, to keep the air pure and to keep the water pure. It considers the sun as the greatest purifier. In places where the rays of the sun do not enter, fire over which fragrant wood is burnt is the next purifier. It is a great sin to pollute water by decomposing matter. Not only is the commission of a fault of this kind sin, but also the omission, when one sees such a pollution, of taking proper means to remove it. On the domestic and social life of the Parsees we find that, according to the teachings of the Parsee books, a husband is the king and the wife the queen of the household. On the husband devolves the duty of maintaining his wife and children; on the wife that of making the home comfortable and cheerful. The qualifications of a good husband, from a Zoroastrian point of view, are that he must be young and handsome, strong, brave and healthy, diligent and industrious so as to maintain his wife and children, truthful, as he would prove true to herself and true to all others with whom he would come in contact, and wise and educated. A wise and intelligent and educated husband is compared to a fertile piece of land which gives a plentiful crop, whatever kinds of seed are sown in it. The qualifications of a good wife are that she be wise and educated, modest and courteous, obedient and chaste. Obedience to her husband is the first duty of a Zoroastrian wife. Marriage is an institution which is greatly encouraged by the spirit of the Parsee religion. It is especially recommended in the Parsee scriptures on the ground that a married life is more likely to be happy than an unmarried one, that a married person is more likely to be able to withstand physical and mental afflictions than an unmarried person, and that a married man is more likely to lead a religious and virtuous life than an unmarried one. The following verse in the Gatha conveys this meaning: ''I say (these) words to you marrying brides and to you bridegrooms. Impress them in your mind. May you two enjoy the life of good mind by following the laws of religion. Let each one of you clothe the other with righteousness because then assuredly there will be a happy life for you.'' An unmarried person is represented as unhappy as a fertile piece of ground that is carelessly allowed to be uncultivated by its owner. Marriage being thus considered a good institution, and being recommended by the religious scriptures, it is deemed a very meritorious act for a Parsee to help his co-religionists to lead a married life. Several rich Parsees have with this charitable view founded endowment funds, from which young and deserving brides are given small sums on the occasion of their marriage for the preliminary expenses of starting in married life. Fifteen is the minimum marriageable age spoken of by the Parsee books. The parents have a voice of sanction or approval in the selections of wives and husbands. Mutual friends of parents or marrying parties may bring about a good selection.

Marriage can be contracted only with persons of their own creed. Polygamy is forbiden except after nine years of sterility, then a man is allowed to marry another woman. Divorces are entirely forbidden. The crimes of fornication and adultery are very severely punished. The women are delicate in frame with small hands; they are fine looking, with brave beautiful black eyes and long hair. They appear somewhat free in public, but take charge of household affairs at home.

When the case of a sick person is hopeless the priest advances to the bed and repeats texts from the sacred book called Avesta, which are to be consolation to the dying man. After death the body is taken to the ground floor where it was born and after being washed and perfumed, and dressed in white, it is laid upon an iron bier. A dog is then brought in to take a last look and thus drive away all the evil spirits. Prayers are said for the repose of the departed soul. All the men friends go to the door, bow down and raise their heads after touching the floor, as an indication of their sorrow for the departed. The body, when put upon the bier, is covered from head to foot, and two men bring it out of the house and give it to four pall-bearers who are dressed in clean white cloths. As they pass with the body all who are present bow to it out of respect. The men friends form a procession with the priests to the Dak-ha-na or "Tower of Silence." These towers are constructed of stone twenty-five feet high, without any entrance except by a ladder to the top. The tower is unroofed. Upon arriving at the tower prayers are said in the prayer house which contains a fire sanctuary. After this the body is placed on a special layer of mortar, where it is exposed. Soon the flesh disappears, being devoured by birds while the skeleton remains. After a certain length of time the bones are removed to a place prepared for keeping them from being exposed to the birds, rain and air. This work must be done in fine clear weather, in case of bad weather the body must be kept until the weather is clear, for which purpose places are provided. When the body is exposed to the birds, etc., there are signs which tell the character of the dead man. If the birds touch the right eye first he was a good man, and if they touch the left eye first then he was a bad man.

Again, on the death of their dear ones, the rich and the poor all pay various sums, according to their means, in charity. These sums are announced on the occasion of the Oothumna or the ceremony on the third day after death. The rich pay large sums on these occasions to commemorate the names of their dear ones.

A child of the Parsees must be born upon the ground floor of the house. That is a requirement of their religion, that its life be commenced in humility and by good thoughts, words and actions. The mother is not to be seen by any one for forty days. After that she washes herself with holy water which has been sanctified by the priest. A Parsee rejects pork, ham and camel flesh, and will not eat anything cooked by one outside of the Parsee religion.

With the overthrow of the Persian monarchy, under the last Sassanian king, Yezdagard, at the battle of Nehavand, in A. D. 642, the religion received a check at the hands of the Arabs, who, with sword in one hand and Koran in the other, made the religion of Islam both state religion and the national religion of the country. But many of those who adhered to the faith of their fathers quitted their ancient fatherland for the hospitable shores of India. Now we have in Persia only about 25,000 Zoroastrians. The Mohammedans called them "guebres," i. e., ungodly. Most of them live in Kerman Yeza, on the soil of the motherland. The men are good citizens, humble, honest and generous, especially to their own brethren, and are also industrious, intelligent, handsome, clean in appearance and faithful to their religion.

THE DEVIL-WORSHIPERS.

The Devil-worshipers dwell in the Monsul Mountains, where they have a church founded in honor of one Mar Ade, who is believed to have been one of the seventy chosen disciples of our Lord. Their chief object of faith and worship is the devil. The world, they believe, belongs to him. He is "the prince of this world," and as such, should be honored and worshiped. They admit that satan is a fallen angel, but hold that in due time God will forgive him ; that he will become converted, and finally be restored to his first estate as the angelic head. What Christ is to the Christians, satan is to these people. They give alms to him and offer sacrifices in his name. They trust in him as the Christians trust in Christ, and believe that he is to be their future mediator and savior of the world. The rooster is regarded by this people as a very sacred fowl, as he is supposed to exactly represent the form of his satanic majesty. In the temple, they keep a golden image of a rooster, which they worship. The priests are an uneducated class of people, not even able to read. They have one book which is called Eljilweh—that means revelation,—but they claim it is a mystery; that no one will be able to understand it until the devil is converted. Their priestly office consists in taking care of the rooster. This golden image, however, is not kept constantly in one place. Some society will offer a certain sum of money for the privilege of keeping it with them for a stated time. After a society has secured the image, it is wrapped in a silk napkin and placed in a very nice basket, overlaid with gold, and thus is carried through the different villages, always accompanied by one priest, no other person being allowed to touch it. We will suppose that they arrive at some village. Immediately the image is set upon some high place, the people come together, bow their heads and worship, while the priest bestows blessings upon them. After this, a napkin is spread at the feet of the image, and upon this the people place their gifts. Much money is collected in this way. A peculiar superstition exists among them. The ground is regarded as most sacred, for it is believed to be the devil's face, and spitting on the ground is regarded as so great a crime that the penalty is death. They are also very careful not to speak satan's name. They call him Melik Taoos. Any missionary is welcomed to their temple, and the people will turn out in large numbers to hear him; but if one single word is uttered beginning with "S," the people will rise up and go out one by one, leaving the missionary alone. They will not pour hot water on the ground for fear of scalding the little devils.

The social customs of these people are peculiar to themselves. Men and women have more freedom of association in their greet feasts. women are permitted to dance and sing with men. The law allows every man to marry not more than six wives; the girl has no freedom to choose her husband. She is virtually sold by the parents like cattle or land. If any girl does not prefer to get married she can remain single at her father's home by paying him a sum of money which she must earn by hard labor. The marriage ceremonies are simple, but accompanied with great feasting. The climax of the wedding is reached as soon as the bride and groom have eaten a loaf of bread made at the home of the Sheikh and brought to them by him. Liquor is freely used by both men and women at the wedding feast. It is customary, when the groom meets his bride, first to throw at her a stone, and she has to bow her head to him, a sign of absolute subjection to his authority. Then he will take a cake of bread and put it over her head, as a sign of her being a merciful woman to the poor and afflicted. It is not legal to consummate marriage during the month of April, that month being considered by them a holy month, nor on any Wednesday or Friday through the year. Women are treated almost like animals, without any rights or respect; their idea of immortality is very degrading. They believe in the transmigration of souls. Altogether they represent a very dark picture. No mission work has ever been attempted among them.

Circumcision is a religious rite but is not rigidly enforced. Once in every forty or fifty years a priest visits the people and circumcises all that are willing. The majority, however, are not circumcised. They bury their dead in a sitting posture facing the temple of their god. They offer yearly sacrifices for their dead. Only one house or family in a community is allowed to be educated, as it is regarded as a sin for every one to have an education. They have no books, but the history of the church is preserved by oral transmission from father to son. They love their religion and are truly devoted and loyal to it. As a people they are very merciful and are faithful in fulfilling all their promises. They borrow and loan money but never take interest. To do this, or even take a pledge or security for a loan is considered a great sin. They consider all nations their enemies except the Syrians. These they regard as brothers. The Kurdish people are their greatest enemies and from these they steal and do not hesitate to kill them. They show no mercy but are cruel and bloodthirsty. These people believe in Christ, but will swear and blaspheme His name. Many of their children are named after Bible characters, such as Isaac, Jacob, Peter and Paul. In 1842 when the Kurds attacked and killed a great many of them they found in their houses a great number of Bibles. In 1883 the British Consul visited Mar Ade, their temple, and their found a golden cross. There is very good evidence to show that many years ago the Christians founded a mission or church at this place, and that these people, although so degenerated, are the descendants of these early disciples.

NESTORIUS.

Nestorious was born near the close of the fourth century at Ger-ma-ni-cia, and was a disciple of Theodore of Neoponestra. He became a Presbyter of Antioch and was made Patriarch of Constantinople in 428. He was distinguished for his fluency of speech and his zeal against prevailing heresies, especially those of the Appollinarians. In his opposition to their doctrine Nestorious maintained that there was a great distinction between Christ as the Son of Man and Christ as the Son of God; that the actions and sensations of the one person were very different from those of the other; that the Virgin Mary could not be called the mother of God, but only the mother of Christ, because it was only the human part of Christ that was born of her, as God is not limited to space, time, location, birth or death. So Nestorius strictly rejected the appellation "Mother of

God" as heathenish and contrary to Hebrew, 7: 3, resting as he did on the orthodox doctrine of the eternal generation of the Son; certainly he could easily say, "A mortal has not given birth to Him, who is not to be created, for in the beginning was the Word;" (as John says); but Nestorious by no means refused to worship the human nature of Christ. He was supported by the eastern bishops in general and by John, bishop at Antioch, in particular, and in the progress of the controversy Nestorius declared himself willing even to adopt the term "Mother of God" if properly explained. Since he was a learned man in literature and an orator of power, Cyril, Patriarch of Alexandria, was jealous of him, he himself desiring to become Patriarch of Constantinople. He attacked the teachings of Nestorious, claiming that he taught that there are in Christ two distinct persons and two natures, and that he denied the divinity of Christ in refusing to call the Virgin Mary the "Mother of God." This criticism of Nestorius' teachings is without foundation, as he did not teach anything of the kind. However, many writers have made this mistake in criticism against the teachings of Nestorius, but we must not forget all the literature in Greek or Latin which his scholars as well as his enemies produced. There are now in the possession of prominent Nestorians manuscripts of Nestorius and his teachings from the seventh century on, and in none of them is that doctrine held. However, his opinions were vigorously combatted by Cyril, Bishop of Alexandria, who, by the advice of Pope Celestine, called a council to Alexandria in 430 to determine the controversy. By this council Nestorius was judged guilty of blasphemy and was anathematized, and Nestorius in turn charged Cyril with confounding the two natures of Christ and anathematized him.

Cyril, being jealous of the Constantinopolitan

bishopric and its great bishop, Nestorius, induced the emperor, Theodosius II, to call a council at Ephesus in 431, at which Cyril presided. As the bishop of Antioch and others from the east had not come as yet, Nestorius refused to appear before the council, as he knew those who were absent were friendly and in harmony with him and his views. But the council again decided against him. Immediately after being deprived of his office, Nestorius withdrew into private life within the monastery of Euprepius, Antioch, until 438, when the emperor ordered his banishment to Petra, Arabia. Later, he was sent to the oasis of Lybia, in upper Egypt. He was still living when Socrates wrote his church history. The time and place, and circumstances of his death are unknown.

Introduction of Christianity among the Syrians or Nestorians.

The origin of the Peshuto Bible (a very early Syrian version) is explained by the following tradition: During the life of Jesus on earth, Abgar, king of Edessa, sent to Jesus a letter inviting him to his city, to escape the persecutions of the Jews, to heal him and to bless his people. Jesus replied that he must remain in Judea, to finish his work, but would after His death and ascension send a disciple, who should heal and teach him. This disciple, being in after years sent and kindly received. The Gospel of Matthew was written in Syriac, and in the course of the second century the rest of the New Testament, save the Second and Third Epistles of John, the Second Epistle of Peter, the Epistles of Jude and James, and the Revelations of Jesust Christ to John. These having not yet been accepted in Canaan as canonical parts of the New Testament, they were translated into what is known as the Peshuto version (it is called Peshuto on account of its simplicity). This version,

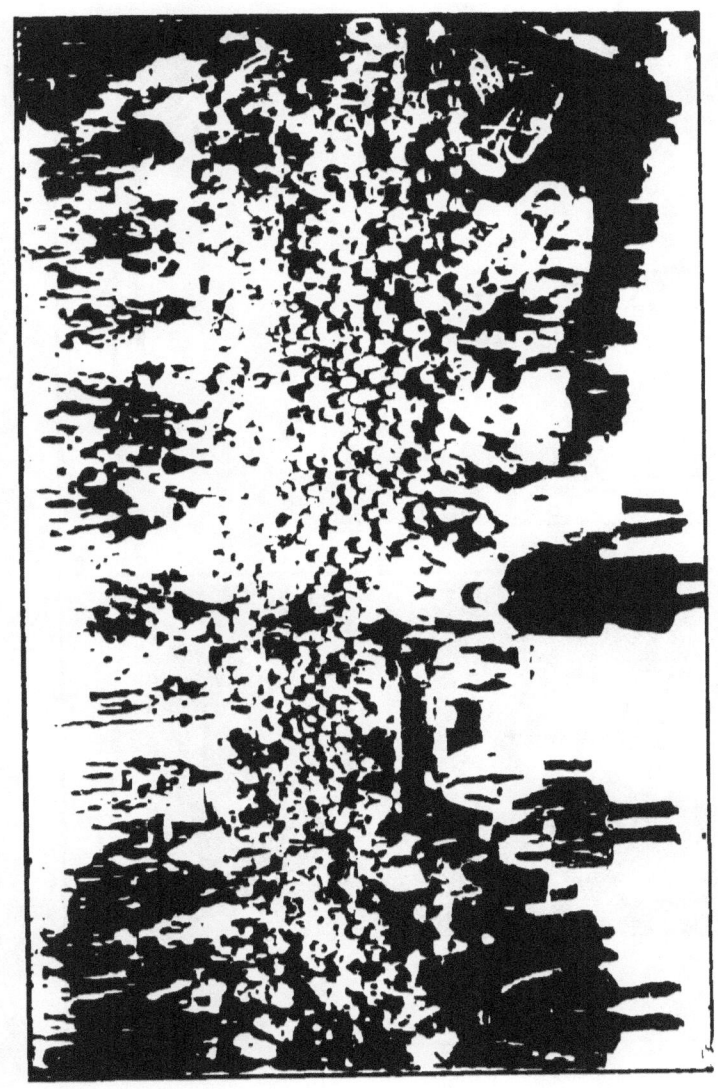

FUNERAL PROCESSION OF JESSE, STEPBROTHER OF THE NESTORIAN PATRIARCH.

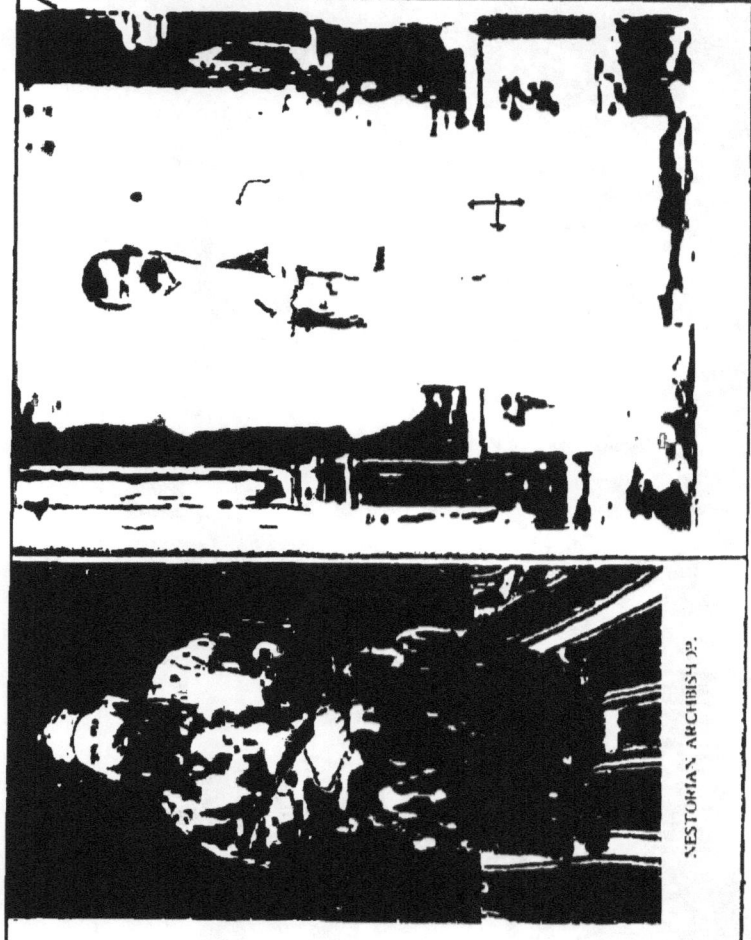

NESTORIAN CLERGICAL COSTUME.

NESTORIAN ARCHBISHOP.

on account of its age, is often cited as high authority upon disputed points.

The Syrian Church was founded in the time when the disciples were scattered by reason of the persecutions, A. D. 44-87, (See Acts 11-19), and by the exertions of the Apostle Paul (Gal.1-21), grew to be one of the most flourishing, and is often mentioned (Acts 13: 1, 15:23, 35:41).

The Syrian Christians were called Martumans from the name Martuma, a missionary from Jerusalem, said to have been one of the Disciples of Christ also " Nazarus," i. e. Nazarene, which name of contempt is in use to-day. Later they were called Nestorians from Nestorius, a Syrian Bishop of Constantinople. (See Nostorius). They were a well organized church, very methodical in matters of government. Their membership was grouped by sevens, forty-nine families under one minister, seven ministers under one Bishop, and seven Bishops under one Metropolitan, all the Metropolitans under one Patriarch. In each year one general synod was held. The character of this church was shown by their building seminaries and colleges. Some of the most important of these were at Nesibia, Oddessa, Urihai, (this was called the queen of the schools), at Antioch and Koochanis. These schools, while they flourished, were the secret of the church's strength. The instructors were the most learned men of their age. Airvaz and St. Basil of Nesibia and Urhai were among the most learned teachers. The Assyrian, Arabic and Greek languages were taught classically. Medicine, astronomy and mathematics, including geometry, were taught. Special attention was given to the study of theology. There were as many as 2,000 monks and students in some of these institutions. There doctors of medicine were given high positions under the Arabian and Persian governments. Literature in the Eastern languages was rich. From these schools came great church fathers, who defended the church from the heretics of the age. The students were prepared for study by some saintly hermit in his cave, they having taken a monastrial vow similar to that of a Nazarete. Next came five years' study in the schools, and that they studied well, is shown by the fact that these men wrote more than 600 commentaries on the Scriptures. Before leaving school each student was expected to make a complete copy of the New Testament, to be left as his gift to the common library. There are to-day in Europe many manuscripts written by these scholars, that are from 300 to 1,200 years old. The New Testament was translated into many dialects by the scholars. These manuscripts are skillfully executed and show the beauty and antiquity of this church. Only a few of these ancient manuscripts are now to be found in Persia and the mountains of Kurdistan, but there are many of them scattered among the libraries of Europe. In these days of printing and typewriting, people have little idea how laborious and beautiful this work was. The earnestness of this church was also shown by the sending of missionaries. Their great work in missions was from the sixth to the thirteenth centuries. They penetrated all Asia and Europe, as is shown by ancient discovery. In China a pillar has been found bearing inscriptions in Chinese and in Syriac: This was written during the reign of Si Coom, Emperor of China, six hundred years after Christ.

Several years ago a Japanese Christian was asked: "To what denomination do you belong?" and answered: "I am a Nestorian," and showed some Nestorian books handed down to him by his forefathers. The instructions given to missionaries are interesting. One of the Bishops, Mar Ephraim (Saint) said: "Change country for country; but from your Master do not change. To every land bring the water of life. In every home to which you come think that you shall find at least one jewel of great price for your Master's treasury and look carefully about, and having found it, spare no pains to bring that soul to the kingdom." The great aim of this school was to educate the monks and to become missionaries and spread the gospel. These schools were fountains from which flowed living waters for a thirsty land. There was no other nation, in their age, that possessed such a spirit of Christian vitality. Zeal for the spread of the Gospel was burning in their hearts as a divine flame. There was a class of Bishops appointed by their leaders to awaken and keep alive this missionary spirit. "The dying love of Christ for sinners," was the text from which they preached. Also His last commission to his disciples, Matt. 28:19-20. These Bishops preached with an inspiration from God and inflamed many hearts until they were ready to sacrifice their lives for Christ. These missionaries wore sandals on their feet, carried a staff of peace in their hands, and a knapsack on their shoulders, containing bread and manuscripts of sacred writings. Thus equipped, they journeyed into heathen lands, following the command of their Nazarene teacher. The church was very poor and had no board of foreign missions to guarantee even a small income. The missionaries went forth trusting in their Heavenly Father. If He took care of the birds in the air, how much more would He care for the heralds of His Gospel. The week before departure was spent in fasting and prayer and consecration. On the last day they partook of communion from the hand of their leader, and solemn advice was given by the bishop. In parting the bishop kissed the missionaries' brow and the latter kissed the bishop's hand and the bishop would say: "The Lord God of the prophets and apostles be with you; the love of Christ defend you; the Holy Spirit sanctify and continually comfort you." Some of the missionaries went to distant lands requiring eight to twelve months to make the journey on foot. They worked in China, India, Tartary, Persia, Beloochhistan, Afghanistan, and northern Africa. Success followed their work. In southern India is a small church planted at that time. These followers are now called the St. Thomas Christians. They always come to Mar Shumon to be ordained as bishops or metropolitans and go back with authority to ordain the lower officers. When I was with the patriarch, in 1895, there were two or more preparing themselves with that view of being ordained or sent among these St. Thomas Christians. A special epistle had been received written and signed by 777 prominent men of those Christians in India, requesting Mar Shumon to send them a metropolitan (as one who had been ordained and sent a few years before, had died), a bishop, two priests, and an interpreter, vouching for the support of these parties and promising help to those who are living in Persia and Turkey. But Mar Shumon could not comply with their request as he had no person who could fill those positions. But the spirit which was stirring as the sun of Heaven began to languish in the tenth century and by the fourteenth century had entirely died, and at present utter ignorance and darkness, and oppression from Mohammedanism and the Catholics prevails. At that time, some of the church's true sons, in lamentation, said: "How are the mighty fallen, and the weapons of war perished!" Hundreds of their missionaries had become martyrs of Christ in a heroic spirit. They would enter fire, singing praises to God, believing their shed blood would be the seed of the church.

In the year 33 after the death of Christ Mar Tuma St. Thomas became Patriarch of the Syrian church. He held the office for five years, and in this time he prepared St. Maree and also St. Eddi, two of the seventy, and St. Thomas, one of the twelve sent out by our Lord Jesus. In 38 St. Thomas went to Hindoostan and St. Maree took his place. St. Maree's residence was in Ktispon on the Tigris, which was for a long time the capital of the Sassanite dynasty. St. Maree expired in A. D. 82. After his death his disciples went to Jerusalem and chose Abriz as their patriarch. He served from A. D. 90 to 107. After Abriz from A. D. 130 to 132, Abraham, a relative of the apostle James, became their patriarch. His successor was James, a just man, and a relative of the Virgin Mary, mother of our Lord. Akhad Abowoy became their patriarch from 205 to 220. During this period there was a severe war between the Romans and Persians. The latter then ruled over Persia, Assyria and Babylonia. The Patriarch of Jerusalem, a subject of Rome, advised the Assyrians who were under the Parthians to elect a Patriarch who was a subject of the Parthians. The Parthians ruled over Persia from 220 B. C. until 226 A. D. In all the changes of government the Assyrians managed to keep in office a succession of patriarchs even to the present time. In the early church down to the year 1405 the Patriarch was chosen by a general vote of the church. Any metropolitan bishop might be chosen. The office held for life. In the year 1405, by reason of great persecutions, the Patriarch, Mar Shimmon, alone was left of all the metropolitans. He therefore appointed one of his own household to succeed him, and thenceforward down to the present day each Patriarch chooses his successors. The choice lies among blood kindred. As a general thing the elder brother is chosen, for there is a rule that the Patriarch must be an unmarried man. Yet in early days of persecution it was sometimes necessary to relax this rule owing to the impossibility of finding in the church a man of sufficient ability who had never been married. The patriarchal city is now Koorchanis. The seat of the Patriarch has been changed from Ktispon to Bagdad, Babel, Ninevah, Mosoel and Elkosh, the town of the Prophet Nahum, and the chief city of learning. Finally in 1778 it changed to Koochanis. The present Patriarch, Mar Shuman, took office in 1865. He is the last of 108 Patriarchs of the Syrian or Eastern Church, whose rule once extended over all Arabia, Hindoostan, China and the mountains of the Caucasus.

Marriage is considered as sacred as the ordination of the clergy, but less sacred than the Lord's supper. Therefore marriage is a solemn service, and the rules relating to it are very strict. Neither of the contracting parties are asked for their assent. When the parents of a son think that it is time for him to be married, they will enquire concerning a young lady among her friends and neighbors as to her character and beauty, and being satisfied in this respect they will notify her parents that they will call upon them. Upon doing this they make their errand known, and if her parents are willing they will kiss the hand of her father. The next morning they will bring a ring and a priest with a large company of friends. Feasting and drinking will be indulged in, the priest will bless the ring and place it on the bride's finger. Promises of dowry will be made by the parents of the bridegroom to those of the bride, also to herself and to her brothers, to the priest of the parish, and to some of her neighbors, who will teach her needle work and embroidery. At the same time they will decide the matter of her dress, and leave enough money to purchase as many suits as are agreed upon. The term of the engagement will vary with the age of the bride. If she be very young the marriage will be delayed some length of time, but if old enough at the time of the engagement the marriage will be consummated at once or in about a month. During the time of the engagement neither of the parties see one another, in fact they may never have met. When the time of engagement expires and the bride's entire outfit is ready, a feast will be proclaimed at both the houses of the bride and bridegroom. The friends of each will go about in the country towns and villages with a drum inviting their friends. They also carry a jug of wine, and in every house they go to they will pour out a glass of it and say, "It is not our wedding, but yours; therefore you are invited to come." After two days of feasting they will send a deputation to the bride's house beating drums and gongs on their way, and having their hands painted red to indicate their happiness. They will sit down to dine at the bride's table while she is preparing herself for the journey to the house of the groom. When the meal is over they will cover her face with coverings and bring her out with a young man on each side of her, one of the young men carrying a purse and a silk handkerchief and running before the procession to announce its coming. When he arrives at the groom's house he stands on the roof together with ten or fifteen young men. These give the groom some wine to drink. The bride is on horseback and is stopped about fifty yards distant from the roof, where the groom is standing. He has three red apples in his hands, and kissing each one, he tries to throw them over the bride, or at her. When the apples strike the ground the crowd of boys will grapple for them, as the supposition is that the boy who gets an apple will be the first one to marry out of the crowd. The rest of the company stands in front of the door, making a hideous noise with their drums and gongs. Sometimes the young men, who are her friends, standing on either side of the horse, will tops the apple with their hands. She will dismount and be brought in, the friends of the young man dancing before her.

The young man is brought down from the roof and brought into the room in the same manner as the bride, and after the feast, the elder of the town will sit in the middle of two rows of guests and placing a napkin on the floor, invite the contributions of those present. He first asks for money from the bride's father, then from any who wish to give. Very often the groom receives on this occasion more money than he has expended in gifts to the bride and her friends. On the next day the marriage ceremony will take place. It is performed by a minister, and a deacon, taken largely from the Bible, and lasts about two hours, during which time the bride and groom remain standing. The bride's dress covers her entire body and face from view except her forehead. She wears a crown and is called a queen. The groom wears a high plume on his crown, fastened to his hat, a sash around his chest and is called a king for about two months. They do not work during this time but take life easy. All the lady friends of the bride will each bring a tray of eatables and they will have a grand feast. It is customary for all the friends to offer gifts of money, gold or silver, in a glass of water. The bride drinks the water and keeps the money. Then they inspect the bride's trunk and see what her father has sent to her and show the presents to all the guests. The bride makes presents of needlework and embroidery, which she has wrought with her own hands, to all the friends. She is kept in close confinement for six months, and does not go out except, perhaps, in the yard or garden. She talks to no one except it be a child. If it becomes necessary to converse with anyone, it must be through a child; she talks to no grown person besides her husband and then only when they are alone. This is continued for eight or ten months, and then she may talk with some of the younger members of the family, but never with the groom's father or mother freely.

Funeral services differ, according to the age of the deceased. As soon as a man dies, word is sent to the priest and deacon. They come to the house of the deceased. The priest will consecrate some water, bathe the body; first the right arm, then the left, then the neck, then the rest of the body. All this time the mourning relatives sing psalms. Then the body is ready to be put into the coffin. The priest and deacon continue singing, the youngest deacon carries the censor and repeats a prayer until they arrive at the grave. Before taking the corpse to the grave, the friends of the deceased come to bid him good-bye. At the grave the priest says a prayer, the body is lowered and the priest takes some earth and sprinkles it upon the coffin, saying: "From earth you came, to earth you return," after which all the people will do the same. While they are filling up the grave, the priest and the deacon continue singing. After this the priest makes a sign of the Trinity on the grave, commencing at the head (which means that Christ came from the Father and descended into the grave.) After the service, the people, being unclean because they have touched the body of a corpse, are taken to a brook and after the priest has blessed the water, they wash their face and hands, then they are cleansed. They now return to the home of the deceased and take two or three meals at the expense of the mourning relatives, while continually repeating: "May God give him rest." After three days they all visit the grave again and the priest again makes the sign of the Trinity, beginning at the foot, (which signifies the resurrection of Christ.) After this all the people shave and bathe and have a great feast to celebrate the close of their time of mourning. After seven days they have another feast and a year later they give offerings and celebrate the Lord's Supper.

Many of their churches are built of stone, while others are made of brick and clay. Some of the buildings are 1300 years old and will stand many years to come. The walls are about eight feet thick at the base, gradually tapering toward the top. In the older churches the doors are quite low and it is necessary for a man to stoop to enter. It is believed by some that the doors were built in this way that the church might be used as a place of refuge, rolling stones in the doorway after entering. Others say the object was to prevent horses, cattle and other animals from entering. These churches are regarded as most sacred places and are called houses of God. There is an interior stairway leading to the roof, which is necessary for repairing the roof or shoveling off snow. The yard in front of a church is shaded with elm trees; it is used as a burial ground. Extending from each corner of the roof is a pair of horns of a wild goat, which is a sign of sacrifice. There is a small room in the rear of the building which is called the most holy place. In this room the priests perform certain ceremonies, and no other people are allowed to enter it at any time. Before this room is a small pulpit on which are placed a cross, Bible and some ceremonial books. The only windows are a few small openings just below the roof. Candles are burned during hours of service to light the room, and incense is burned as a ceremonial and to produce a pleasing odor. There are no pictures on the walls, but there are some decorations in the way of finely embroidered silk draperies donated by some of the worshipers. Reading Scripture and prayer book and chanting Psalms are the main features of worship. There is no music except a number of small bells on the walls, which the worshipers ring as they enter the building. The audience sits on the floor or stands through the service. Assyrians believe the two chief ordinances to be the Lord's supper and baptism. The ordaining of priests and marriage are ordinances that rank next in importance. Baptism is administered by bishops and elders. All the children of a member are baptized by immersion. Some believe that baptism regenerates a child, while others say it will have a good effect, provided the parents give the child proper training thereafter.

The Lord's Supper is administered with much ritual on festival days, such as Easter, Christmas and Ascension Day. This ceremony is more highly honored than any other ordinance, as it commemorates the death and victory of Christ. Both wine and bread are used. A few years ago, and even now in some places, it was a custom to make the bread and wine from gleanings brought in from the field and vineyards by virgins. This was considered pure and most acceptable as it had belonged to no man. They do not believe with the Catholics that the bread and wine are turned into the flesh and blood of Christ, but they put much emphasis on these ingredients after the same have been consecrated. They are then holy. On the night previous to communion day the priests and deacons go to the church shortly after midnight, and entering into the most holy place, make the bread for use on the next day. The priest himself kneads the dough. This bread is considered more sacred than that made in the ordinary way. After the bread has been made the remainder of the night is spent in chanting Psalms, reading the Scriptures and prayer book. An hour before sunrise the people flock to church. When the church is full of worshipers the priest mounts the pulpit, chants the sacred words for an hour or more, the audience remaining in perfect silence until he reaches the end of a Psalm or the end of the service, when all respond "Amen." The priest and a deacon stand in the pulpit to administer the sacrament. Communicants come forward one by one, and the priest puts a small piece of bread in their mouths and the deacon gives the wine. Children under 7 years of age do not partake of the sacrament. On these occasions the priest and deacon wear long white robes of silk or cotton tied about the waist with a long silk girdle. A turban is worn on the head.

Their faith, as described in some ancient manuscripts, is purely evangelical. They believe in the trinity, God the Father, Son and Holy Ghost. These three persons are co-equal, co-eternal, unmixed and inseparable. Their clergy does not claim the power to forgive sins. They accept the apostle's creed and it is recited by the clergy and religious men. They deny the confession, image worship and doctrine of purgatory. But the church has fallen into decay under the persecutions of Mohammedans, and they now in their ignorance worship souls or pray to the saints. They have adopted much of the Roman Catholic heresies; many days of fasting are observed, as fifty days before Easter, twenty-five days before Christmas, every Friday and Wednesday and others. During these fasts the old people take no food until noon. On these fasting days the people will abstain from meats or fatty foods, etc. In times of persecutions their schools and books were destroyed and the people became ignorant, at the same time the Catholics introduced among them their literature, which changed their prevailing doctrines.

BABISM.

The Mohammedan religion is today divided into about fifty different sects, and this division greatly weakens it. Within fifty years past a new religion has been developed in Persia, known by the name of Babism, which already numbers its disciples by hundreds of thousands, and is steadily making inroads upon the

Mohammedan religion of which it is in fact an offshoot. It is thought by some to have a large future before it. Christian missionaries come in contact with it, and from the friendliness of the so-called Babis to the Christian religion hopes have been cherished, that it may prove a stepping stone for the Gospel into Moslem hearts. For this reason, if no other, it deserves the attention of all thoughtful Christians. Mirza Ali Mohammed, the founder of the new religion, was the son of a cloth merchant of the city of Shiraz, and first came to public notice in the year 1843. He began to plan the new religion at the age of 18, but did not reveal it until he was 25 years old. The foundation of his faith was this: Mohammed like Christ, taught that the latter days will be a millennium. They have a tradition that when all prophets have died or have been killed by their enemies, a son six years of age will, by the direction of Allah, be hid in an unknown well. He is to remain there until the millennium. It was believed that he would be the ruler of the Mohammedans in these last days. He was to lead both his victorious armies and conquer all the world, and Islam would become the universal religion. His early education was limited even for the advantages Persia affords, but with a strong spiritual bent in his nature he seems to have given himself much to religious meditation and study. Paying a visit to Kerbela, the center of theological thought among the Shiahs of Persia, he sat for a few months under the teaching of a noted and rather mystical teacher of the Mohammedan theology and became his enthusiastic disciple. He entered with special zest into the study of the doctrine which figures so conspicuously in Persian theology, of the coming "Unseen Imam" whose return as the "Imam Mahdi" is to introduce the Mohammedan millennium, in regard to whom some advanced and heretical views were taught by the school to which his teacher belonged. The impressions made on his mind by his devout contemplations on this doctrine are exhibited in the following passages which we find translated from his earlier writings : Addressing the absent Imam he says :

When are the days of your empire, that I may struggle for you ? And when are the days of your glory, that I may obtain the blessings of your visage ? And when are the days of your kingdom, when I may take revenge on your enemies ? And when are the days of your manifestation, that I may be independent of all except you ? And when are the days of the appearance of your lordship, that by your permission I may say " Be," and it shall become existent before you ? And when are the days which God has promised unto his servants for your coming?

From his long and earnest meditations on this subject, he seems to have become convinced that he enjoyed the favor of special communication with the Imam. It was but one step farther to imagine that his axalted thoughts were veritable inspirations from the supreme fountain of all truth, and that he, himself, was an inspired prophet. Upon his return from Karbela, the young enthusiast drew about him his particular friends, and revealed to them his inward consciousness of a prophetic call, announcing himself as the " Bab," i. e., the door, or gate, meaning the channel of grace from the unseen Imam. He began preaching in the mosques against the prevailing irreligion of the times, especially berating the Moslem clergy for their scandalous vices and unfitness to be spiritual guides to the people, emphasizing the need of a morality of deeds, rather than one of words and formal rules. He advocated temperance, opposed the growing use of opium— while he, himself, neither smoked tobacco nor drank liquor or coffee. He discountenanced polygamy, forbade concubinage, asceticism and mendicancy, prohibited divorce and taught the equality of the sexes; encouraged the practice of hospitality, and demanded justice for all citizens alike. Though attacking none of the dogmas of Islam, the tendency of his opinions were undeniably heterodox. The new teachings, however, became popular at once. Numbers of his fellow citizens assented to the pretensions and creed of the new claimant to prophethood with alacrity and fervor. Missionaries were sent out to other towns to announce the tidings, and explain the new doctrines. Adherents sprang up everywhere they went—men of all ranks, educated and unlearned alike welcoming the good news, and in turn becoming their earnest heralds. This great popularity was due not merely to the attractive program of reform presented, but largely to the personal sanctity conceded to the Bab, a quality to which the Oriental mind is ever particularly susceptible, to the sweetness of his manners, to the eloquence of his voice and to the apparent depth of meaning in his utterances, all of which exercised a spell over his hearers even his enemies admitted and feared. In stature, he was tall and slender, eyes black, eye-brows heavy and long, beard patriarchal. His countenance was very pleasant and attractive. In conversation with high and low classes of people alike, he showed himself a servant of all. He was poetical, a great orator and a deep thinker. He wrote many beautiful poems. His epistles to his disciples were philosophical. His words in sermons touched the hearts of men. Later on, Mirza Ali Mohammed, like a good Moslem, made a pilgrimage to Mecca. His return was signalized by the renewal of debates and dissensions between himself and his followers on the one side and the orthodox party on the other, which finally led to the arrest of the Bab by the governor of his native province and his detention at Shiraz for a time. Subsequently he was removed to Ispahan, where a friendly governor showed him much favor. Meanwhile, his apostles continued more active in their proselyting work than ever. Notable among these were two of the regular Mohammedan clergy of great learning and ability, who rank in the history of this movement as the foremost champions of the new doctrines—Mullah Hussein and Haji Mohammed Ali. With these was associated a woman, who has obtained a celebrity throughout Persia almost unparalleled in the annals of that land. She is admitted by friend and enemy to have been a woman of marvelous beauty and rare intellectual gifts. As a scholar, she excelled in her knowledge of the Arabic language and of Islamic traditions and philosophy. She was a poetess, and her eloquence of speech was fascinating. Her name was Zerryn Taj, but she is commonly known as Kurratul-Ayn, or "the Consolation of the eyes," with reference to her surpassing lovliness of countenance. She never met the Bab during her lifetime, but learned of him as a spiritual guide and channel of the new revelation through Mullah Hussein. From her correspondence with the Bab, he became impressed with her rare qualities and attainments, and included her as one of the eighteen dignitaries of the first Babi Hierarchy. In the campaign that was pushed by the devotees of the Bab, the persuasive eloquence of this peerless young Persian woman is credited as second to that of no other.

By degrees the new sectarians became more and more bold, more and more sanguine of revolutionizing the ancient faith of the land. In all the principal cities of central and southern Persia, some in every class in society, publicly or privately, hailed the reform movement as a welcome change in the old order of things. The orthodox clergy became alarmed as they saw their religious supremacy in danger of dissolution, while the turmoils and insurrections which followed from the Babi preachers, opened the eyes of the government to serious danger to state as well as church. In the

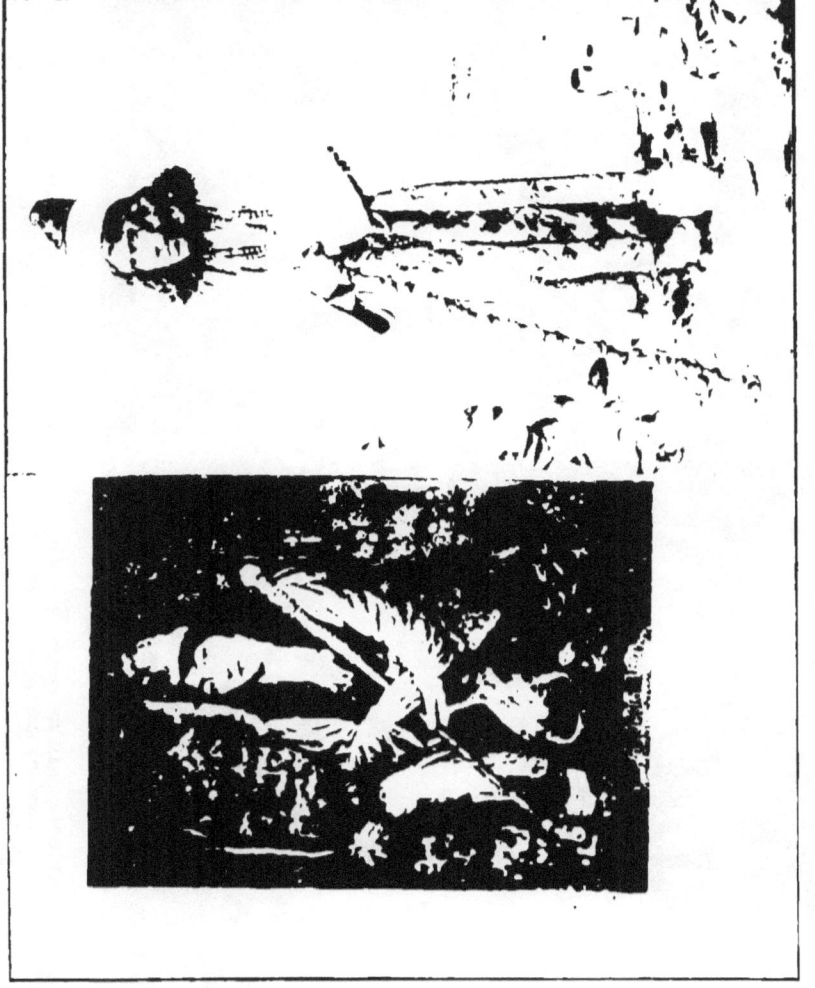

CONFIRMATION OF A YOUTH AMONG   PRIEST OF FIRE-WORSHIPERS ATTEND-
THE FIRE-WORSHIPERS.   ING TO HOLY FIRE.

provinces of Khorassan and Mazanderan and in the city of Zenyan, the Babis, assumed a fierce and defiant front coming into violent collision with the local authorities. The king's ministers, as the first steps toward checking the rising tide of revolution, ordered the Bab to be removed from Ispahan to Tabriz and there secluded in some safe place. This was in the year 1847, only four years since the youthful Ali Mohammed first announced his prophetic mission. On arriving at Tabriz he was despatched by order of the governor to the fortress of Maku, held by a semi-independent chieftain, situated at the base of Mt. Ararat, three or four days to the north-west of Tabriz; but his confinement there was not so close as to prevent the access of his friends and an active correspondence with distant and industrious lieutenants. To interrupt this freedom of communication, he was removed to the fortress of Cherick near Salmas, two days from Oroomiah. The quiet of his retirement here lasting two years and a half, was favorable to medita-tion and study and he busied himself in practices of devotion and in the developement of his theological opinions and his code of civil and social regulations. Gradually he assumed higher and higher position and authority, until he announced himself to be the "Iman Mahdi," himself. During this interval the religious war kindled by the Bab's energetic followers in Mazan-deran and Zenyan grew into a blaze, which taxed all the energies of the local governments to extinguish. Meanwhile, Mohammed Shah died (September 5, 1848) and was succeeded by his son, Nasreddin, the late sovereign of Persia, who selected as his prime minister the very able statesman Mirza Taki Khan. Immedi-ately upon coming into power, this minister addressed himself vigorously to quelling the Babi disturbances in different districts and towns. That in the town of Zenyan, where the Bab's friends were very numerous and resolute, was only put down after a prolonged siege, lasting from May to September, 1850. While the contest dragged on, the government determined on the death of the Bab, as absolutely necessary to the pacification of the kingdom. On his way from the castle of his imprisonment to Tabriz for trial and execution he passed through Oroomiah. We are told that vast numbers flocked to see him, and even the governor did not conceal his sympathy with the prisoner of such engaging manners; the crowd shed tears as they looked upon the interesting young man, and more than half believed that he might be the very "Imam Mahdi," the great desire of Moslem nations. Traditions, about the town, relate that when he went to the bath the people carried away the water in vessels, in which he had bathed as if it were holy. But at Tabriz, Persian officialdom and the sternly orthodox populace of that city, did not so lose their heads. The man was examined before the Moslem high priests and was condemned, as a heretic, to be shot, along with two of his companions in arrest. One of these, however, recanted and saved his life. The Bab was conducted from one priest's house to another in succession, each in turn ratifying the sentence of death, while in the crowded streets through which he passed, throngs of zealous fanatics grossly insulted him and his companion. Arriving at the place of execution, a public square in the city, the prisoners were suspended by their arms against a wall, in conspicuous public view and a company of soldiers were drawn up to shoot them.

At the first discharge the Bab's companion fell dead, but strange to say, the bullets only cut the cords which bound the Bab himself, leaving him fall to the ground, free, and he took to flight. It is thoroughly conceivable, indeed it is altogether probable, from a Persian point of view, that had the man risen and thrown himself upon the confidence of the superstitious populace,

declaring his delivery a miracle of divine power in his
favor, and a confirmation of his claims, the whole town
would have acclaimed his pretensions and sooner or later
the country itself would have acknowledged his authority
to overthrow the Kajar dynasty. As it was, in his be-
wilderment, he fled to a neighboring guard house where
he was cut down and beaten to death by Mussulman
soldiery. This occurred July 15, 1850. The execution
of the Bab in no wise discouraged the faith and zeal of
his disciples; on the other hand, it exasperated them
against the government and inflamed them to desperate
efforts for its overturn. By the vigorous efforts of the
military power the several insurrections in the country
were brought to an end. But the spirit of vengeance
for the death of their prophet was everywhere rife
among the sect and soon came to a head in the conspir-
acy against the life of the Shah. He was attacked
while riding out with his suite one day by three Babis.
The attempt was a failure the king escaping with only
a slight wound, but the recoil of the blow on the Babis
was terrible. One of the assailants was killed on the
spot, the other two were tortured with fiendish cruelty
to induce them to reveal their fellow conspirators, but
without avail. Some thirty residents of the capitol
were suspected of being Babis, were seized and after a
month's deliberation on the part of the Shah and his
court, they were put to death in a variety of methods
the most cruel and barbarous, large numbers of the
nobility, the ecclesiastics and other citizens of Teheran
being forced to aid in their execution in evidence of
their loyalty to the Shah. Among the victims was the
gifted woman Kurra'l-Ayn, who for some months had
been under arrest and surveilance in the city. All the
victims met their death with stoical, almost superhu-
man fortitude, refusing the pardon offered them if they
would but recant. Some even in the midst of their

prolonged sufferings sang or shouted songs of triumph
The French writer Renau speaks of this massacre,
as a day "without parallel" perhaps in the history of
the world. It should be borne in mind that some of
these unfortunates had never seen the man whom they
called master, yet thus rapturously did they offer up
their lives as a testimony of their faith in him. This
ferocity of vengeance checked, though it did not by any
means extripate Babism. While it put an end to the
revolutionary tendencies of its more restless spirits
secret partisanship continued to keep alive the heresy.
Two brothers who stood foremost among the sect,
one of whom had been nominated by the Bab as his successor, found it safe to escape over into Turkey and
made their residence for some years in Bagdad. Here
their abodes became centers of rival missionaries efforts,
from which the Persian rulers took alarm, and at their
earnest request the Osmanli government ordered their
removal to European Turkey; and finally one of them,
Mirza Yahya, was sent to the island of Cyprus, where
he still lives; the other, Mirza Husein Ali, was removed
to Acre, a Turkish stronghold on the Mediterranean
coast.

According to the Bab no divine revelation is final.
His was the latest, but not the last manifestation of the
deity in human form. There are numerous passages in
his writings which intimate that he is but the forerunner
of One to come. The expression frequently occurs, "He
whom God shall manifest." His followers have never
been agreed as to the exact meaning of this phrase.
The prisoner at Acre came to interpret it as referring
primarily to himself, and boldly claimed that he was
the one predicted, setting aside the Bab's nomination of
his brother to the headship. The larger portion of the
Babis have come to acknowledge his claims, yielding to
him divine homage. He assumed the name of Beha,

i. e., Light. Often he is designated as "Beha 'Ullah," or "Light of God," and his followers are known as Behais as well as Babis. The younger brother is commonly known as Subhi-Ezel, i. e., "Light of Eternity," and his disciples are called Sub-i-Ezelis. Though the Beba proclaimed himself to be the divine being incarnate, he made no pretense of working miracles, but like the Arabian prophet and like the Bab, he offered as proof of his claims simply and alone the superlative excellence of his compositions. Up to the time of his recent death he resided in no small degree of comfort at Acre in a mansion encompassed by orange groves furnished him by the Turkish government, numerous Persian attendants surrounding the place carefully guarding all approach of strangers to their revered master, keeping up an air of impressive awe as was supposed to befit the abode of so exalted a personage. In his writings more is made of himself and his own teachings than of the Bab and his prescriptions. Among other products of his pen are noticeable several letters addressed to sovereigns of Europe and Asia and to the President of the United States, in which he appeals, as by divine authority, for the cessation of wars, for international comity and good feeling, for the prevalence of justice and righteousness, and for the recognition of his claims as the present representative of God on earth. Since his death it is not known what position is taken by his followers with respect to a successor, but up to the present time the Behais have been gaining converts widely throughout Persia. He taught that every age must have its own prophet inspired from God. He claimed that he was inspired and that he had frequent communications from God telling him how to direct the people. He openly claimed to be the Imam, and he taught that the priesthood and the religion were corrupt and that he was appointed to renew them. He did not oppose the Koran, but at the same time said that every age needs a new Bible. He claimed to have received a Bible from God.

This book is called Bayon, meaning exposition. He taught the equality of both sexes and paid homage to woman. He showed that it was against the law of God to marry more than one woman or to keep concubines. Further, it is against the law of society and the happiness of women for man to have more than one wife. The law of divorce, which is common among Mohammedans, was not practiced by the new sect. The place of women among them is the same as among Christians. The prophet taught that the spirit of charity ought to be as a flame of fire in the hearts of his followers. He said we cannot please God if we see our brother in need and do not help him; if we pray He will not hear us, if we worship Him He will turn his face away from us. Believing this, the spirit of charity is very strong among them and they support the needy. The use of wine and all intoxicants is strictly forbidden. They are very kind to people of other faiths who are not Mohammedans, them, they hate. The Babis charge the Christians with Jewish blindness in not recognizing their prophet as the returning Christ, with a new Gospel. But no true Christian can study the principles of Babism without a painful conviction of its entire unworthiness to be called a Gospel in any sense. It is a system of crude, mystical ideas, barren of all spiritual value to humanity. Religion is made by it to consist chiefly in the worship of God as manifested in the assumed incarnations. Nothing, scarcely, is taught of the Divine Holiness, nor of sin, nor of repentance; nothing of Divine love, nor of a Savior, nor of holy living. The principles of morality inculcated are indeed somewhat higher than those current among the Moslems and emphasis is laid on sincerity, as all essential in religion, a quality conspicuously absent with the Shiahs, but in fact the followers of the Beha pay slight heed to these nobler teachings while they seize eagerly upon the freedom granted them from the exactions of Mohammedan law. They neither fast nor pray except, possibly, the latter over the dead; they are addicted to wine drinking, even to excess. As to the doctrine of the equality of men and women which the Bab enjoined, it is but partially maintained in practice, and the same may be said in respect to other of his teachings intended to elevate the position of woman. Indeed, what valuable fruit could we expect from a religious system which argues against creation and the resurrection, which has no adequate conception of the nature of sin, presents no higher motive to goodness than the extinction and final absorption of the human soul into the Divine Being, and holds up no fear of punishment nor serious loss to transgressors of the moral law. It is indeed amazing, that men are so ready to devote themselves to death, at the hands of their enemies, for a system of religious beliefs so empty of all practical benefit. The enmity between them and the orthodox Mohammedans has been very severe. From the killing of Bab until the present time, they have been trying to kill the Shah. In their first attempt they failed, but May 1, 1896, while the Shah was worshiping in the most holy place of the mosque, he became the victim of a fanatic Babi who had disguised himself as a woman. This Babi, while under disguise, shot the king, who died two minutes afterwards. Some thought the government would again persecute them, but there were some hindrances which would not permit this. In the first place their religion is kept a secret; it is impossible to know who belongs to the new sect. Secondly, many of the high classes and royal officers belong to this sect, and for this reason it would be impossible to persecute them. Thirdly, their number today would reach

2,000,000, or about that, and to kill this enormous company would certainly damage the government.

Their antagonism against the government, and against orthodox Mohammedism, is caused entirely by the lack of freedom of religious worship. We cannot regard it other than wild fanaticism : and the worst of it is, that it is fanatacism which has instigated some of its followers to the assassination of its adversaries, giving color to the prediction of many that, if the Babis should ever attain to a position of political power, they would prove the most intolerant and vengeful of all sects. Our sympathies can but go out to them, for the terrible sufferings which they have undergone in behalf of what they hold to be the truth, and above all their pitiful blindness and folly. The chief virtue to be laid to their credit is their mutual devotion and fraternal affection. This, and the religious liberty they practice, are the chief ties that bind them together as a sect, and in these, doubtless, lies the secret of their constant growth. They are very warm friends of the Christians, placing in them the greatest confidence; sometimes they will even lodge in the houses of Christians, and eat with them without questioning. This a strict Mohommedan would never do. They readily allow the Christian to preach to them and to discuss religion with them. Yet it is not an easy matter to convert them, for one must know their manner of life and religious doctrines too successfully meet their arguments. A few, however, have been truly converted. This filled the Mohammedans with hatred, both against the Christians and the converts. When the Christian shows the superiority of Christ, and of His doctrine, over that of their Prophet Bab, they are forced into silence. They are now securing many converts from Mohammedism, and it is believed that the time will come when reilgious toleration will be obtained by them. This will also give the Christians a good opportunity of preaching the Gospel. It is a matter of some hopefulness to the Christian that these people listen to the Gospel with the greatest readiness, and consequently by reading with them it seems possible to lead them to see the errors into which they have fallen. There is greater encouragement to missionary effort in the fact that these people are everywhere undermining or relaxing the orthodox Moslem belief, and so are opening the doors of conscience and faith among the Mohammedans to the saving truths of the Gospel of the Crucified Son of God.

CONCLUSION.

The title of our work dedicated to the furtherance of the Gospel in Persia is " Darkness and Daybreak." Paul speaks of the night being far spent, and the day is at hand, with those who are deeply interested in the concerns of the Gospel and the light, it reveals with respect to the Kingdom of God and the glory manifested in Jesus Christ. There is anxiety to be instrumental in casting off the works of darkness which is blinding many, through the prince of darkness, whether in the form of a formal religion or open idolatry, deluding the simple into the fatal errors which, unless by the the consecrated efforts of Christ and his Church, must perish for lack of knowledge. With this hope in view, I make an appeal to you all, God willing, to lend me your prayers and assisting heart and hand to carry on the work now begun in Persia. Have we not need, every one of us who profers the name of our Lord Jesus Christ, to put on the armor of light, to be clothed in this armor and go forth in the field that God has in his kind and loving providence opened for us.

Letter received from my brother Joseph while in prison at Dixxa, Gavar, Turkey, stating that my message had reached him, and British and American ambassadors had been informed and every effort was being made to secure my release, etc.

واٸزه انكليز قونسلى موستزهالورت
جابلوٸنه امريقا تبعه سنك نسطورب
ملتدن مشعونك كوريشنه كيدن موستر
اٸراك ادمز پساپورطنى شهبندروكيلذن
تصديق ايدرٸمش ايكن كواٸده پساپورطى
الوب خٸس ايدلمش مومااليهه معاوننزب
رجا ايدرم انكلتره موسيوزلرنذن نيسان
دراروۑ

Telegram of English missionary sent to British Consul at Van, Turkey,
requesting his aid for the release of Isaac Adams,
sent June, 1895.

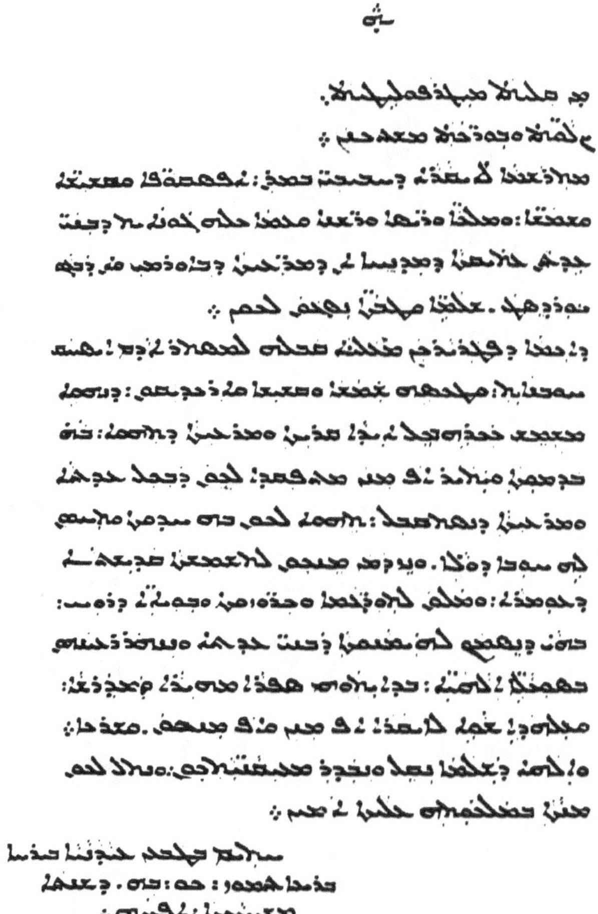

Ordination Diploma, from Mar Knanishu, a Nestorian Metropolitan, conveying the privilege to preach and teach among Nestorians and be kindly and respectfully received by them.

BELOVED IN THE LORD:

For the purpose of more effectively propagating the mission in Persia, already begun by means of establishing a number of Christian schools, distributing Bibles and other Christian religious literature, etc., we are in sore need of a printing press of moderate capacity. It would by this be brought within our reach to furnish a sufficient quantity of Bibles, whole or in part, catechisms, tracts, etc., to cover all parts of Persia, Kurdistan and the Caucausus, which could scarcely ever be made possible so long as such books, etc., must be bought from dealers. My brother, Abraham Adams, having spent some time in this country for the particular purpose of learning the printers' trade, has now returned to Persia ready to take this branch of our mission work. Allow me, therefore, to present to you an appeal in behalf of our work, and most especially this part of it, the purchase of a small printing press.

Considering this appeal, look not at yourself, and your wants and needs, but at Christ, with all His riches and wealth. He has made many promises which he can and will fulfill. Of course, he can and will help our work along, in spite of any or many persons' ill will, as it has been begun and is propagated in His name; but is it not a dear privilege of yours, who call yourself after his name, to be permitted to aid in maintaining and furthering it? Christ wants the Gospel spread and His kingdom extended on earth by Christians, for to His disciples He has given the command to go and teach all nations. And do you not remember that your dear Lord and Master has promised a reward for all that you do in His name, even to handing a draught of cold water to the thirsty? What a blessed sensation it will create in every giver to read or to learn that the mission in Persia is progressing finely, and that it had been brought about to a great extent by the gifts of those Christians, who made it possible to buy a printing press, by means of which the Gospel was made to penetrate places heretofore considered unpenetrable.

But you are too poor to give anything? It is often the case, that dear Christians refrain from giving for a certain purpose because they think they cannot give enough. This is a sad mistake.

The mite you give helps the cause along and is in the eyes of the Lord, who can easily make much out of little, a means perhaps, to do great good, which, should you but be able to perceive it, would astonish you to the utmost. But you cannot give anything? Yet you can aid our work if you will. You are a Christian? If so, you cannot help to pray. When you pray, think of the poor Mohammedans, Kurds, Devil-Worshipers and Fire-Worshipers in Persia; think of the poor Nestorians, who consider themselves Christians and yet do not know their Lord and Savior Jesus. This sad affair lay before Him in your prayer and ask Him, fervently, to help the mission in Persia along. When you say amen, He also will say, amen, yea, so shall it be. I thus leave this appeal to your prayerful consideration, trusting that you will not shrink from doing something for this cause.

Gifts towards the purchasing of a printing press or towards the benefit of the Persian mission in general, please send to

ISAAC ADAMS,
Oroomiah, Persia,
via Berlin and Odessa,

Or No. 124 Lagrave St ,
Grand Rapids, Mich. U. S. A.

The following are a few of the many testimonials I have covering a period from June 11, 1890, to April 8, 1898:

Mr. Adams spoke to a large and deeply interested congregation at the First Reformed Church, on Sunday, March 4, 1894.

Mr. Adams gives an impression of sincere and devoted zeal to spread the knowledge of the Redeemer among his unfortunate fellow-countrymen in Persia. and, therefore, we take just pleasure in recommending him as in every way worthy of sympathy and respect.   W. H. WILLIAMSON, Pastor,
Grand Rapids, Mich.

This is to certify that the Rev. Isaac Adams, of Persia, spoke to my people on the evening of Thursday, September 20, 1894, and that we all were much edified by his words, and wished many more had heard him. He is a native of Persia, who has been in this country some three years, more or less, preparing himself to preach the Gospel to his countrymen. He took a course in Mr. Moody's Training School, at Chicago, and sent home to bring his three brothers to this country, that they too might receive a Christian education. Before Mr. Adams' coming to us I received high recommendations of him, as a sincere Christian, from several of the western brethren. among whom were Revs. Winter, of Grand Rapids, Birchby, of Holland, De Bruyn, of Grand Haven, and Ihrman, of Marion. Through an oversight those letters were lost, but all of them expressed unqualified confidence in Brother Adams as a true Christian and able speaker.

We learned in a few hours to regard him very highly in love for his work's sake, and our church will always be open to welcome him. He is not working under any of our boards, but all who have met him concur in the impression that he is one of the Master's workers, whose Christian fellowship it is a privilege to possess   JOHN G. GEBHARD,
Pastor Reformed Church, Herkimer, N Y.

Mr. Adams, a native of Persia, who has been five years in this country and soon goes back to labor among his own people, spoke last evening to our people and greatly interested them. They gladly gave him their sympathy and substantial assistance.

Mr. Adams came with abundant testimonials, and I gladly add my own expression of confidence and personal interests. He speaks English as well as need be.
EDWARD G. SELDEN, D. D.,
Pastor Madison Ave. Reformed Church, Albany, N. Y.

I take pleasure in saying Mr. Isaac Adams gave an interesting and instructive address in our lecture room, on the evening of September 26, 1894. His use of the English language is very good and his subject matter can not fail to please.

Mr Adams is an earnest young man and we wish him abundant success in his proposed work.

THOMAS POWELL VERNOLL,
Pastor First Reformed Church, Paterson, N. J.

This is to certify that I am personally acquainted with Mr. Isaac Adams, and have every confidence in his Christian character and honesty of purpose. He is preparing himself, by study, to the missionary work in his native land of Persia. Any help rendered him in securing places to lecture, etc , will be worthily bestowed. C. PERRIN, Ph. D., Pastor,
We concur :   Chicago, Ill.
B. F. JACOBS, (Great Sunday school man).
W. R. HARPER, Ph. D., President University of Chicago.

I very cordially commend Mr. Isaac Adams to the Christian public. He is a native of Persia, belongs to the old Nestorian stock, has the highest testimonials from those who have intimately known him in his own land and in this. I have seen enough of him to satisfy me that he is an earnest and humble Christian. His lectures have been uniformly listened to with pleasure and profit. I trust that he may be cordially welcomed and helped in his work of preparation for the service to which he hopes to devote his life. P. S. HENSON, D. D.,
Pastor First Baptist Church, Chicago, Ill.

I am more than pleased with the acqaintance I have had with Mr. Isaac Adams, and our people were much interested and edified with the address which he gave April 9, 1893, in the church. I most sincerely pray the richest blessing of God upon his life.
J. A. JOHNSTON, D. D ,
Pastor First Baptist Church, Kalamazoo, Mich.

To WHOM IT MAY CONCERN : Mr. Isaac Adams addressed a meeting at the First Baptist Church with great acceptance. He is a very entertaining and instructive speaker, and the spirit of his lecture is exceptionally good It gives me great pleasure to cordially commend him to the churches.
J W. CONLEY,
Pastor First Baptist Church, St. Paul, Minn.

May it be known to you who meet this letter, that we have accepted the plan of the Rev. Mr. Isaac Adams, which is to engage himself in the educational works of our people and other needs that they have.

We appointed him to teach according to the doctrine and faith of Mar-Marai, Mar Adai and St. Thomas the Blessed Apostles and Founders of the Ancient Church in the East, and of the Scriptures, without any change or alteration in all their requirements. It is upon these conditions that we set our seals, the Chieftains of the Ancient Chaldean Church of the East.

The Grace of our Lord Jesus Christ be with you all, amen.

Written at the See House by Priest Eshoo, the Secretary of the Patriarch, June 15, 1895.

Translated from the original by the Rev. Prof. Abr. Yohannan, Columbian College, New York.

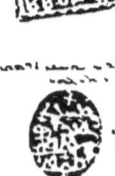

July 10, 1895

To All Whom it May Concern: Mr. Isaac Adams addressed the Central Baptist people, Sunday evening, June 4, 1893, and gave a most interesting description of Persian manners and religious beliefs. His knowledge is ample and his ability to set it before others in a pictorial manner is quite unusual His lecture is both entertaing and instructive. To grant him the privilege of addressing a congregation is a favor to the people fully as much as to him. Besides this, he is of worthy character and merits sympathy in his efforts to obtain an education. I do not usually write letters like this, but say these words heartily.

REV. CHAS. A REESE,
Pastor Central Baptist Church, Minneapolis, Minn.

Mr. Isaac Adams gave an interesting address on above date. Mr. Adams speaks English remarkably, considering his short time in this country; is preparing himself to return to his native land as a missionary; is dependent upon his addresses for his support and expenses at school. Help him.

REV. MANLY BENSON,
Grimsby Park, Ontario, Canada.

Mr. Isaac Adams spoke at our missionary concert on Persia, its religion and people, to the great delight of our people. Would advise any pastor to give him a hearing.

REV. WAYLAND HOYT, D. D.,
Pastor First Baptist Church, Minneapolis, Minn.

Isaac Adams, or, in his own language, "Ishak Adam," seeks to fit himself for the work of a missionary in Persia, and I have reason to believe he is worthy of all the help we can render.

REV. RICHARD S MARTIN, D. D.,
Grace M. E. Church, Chicago. Ill.

A large congregation greeted Mr. Isaac Adams in our church Sunday evening, March 12, 1893, and listened with great pleasure and profit to his address on Persia, etc Had he continued to speak each night during the week I am persuaded he would have had full houses On the evening of March 14, through a blizzard, many went to Montague to hear him, and there, where he has spoken several times, the house was crowded. No minister need hesitate to make way for him. He will do the people of any community good and help the cause of christianity; especially awakening an interest in missions. I most heartily endorse him

ALBERT SMITH,
Pastor M. E. Church, Whitehall, Mich.

To Whom it May Concern: This is to say that Mr Isaac Adams spoke to the people of the Woodward Avenue Baptist Church, Wednesday evening, May 10, 1893, and greatly interested them in the story of the religion of his native country and the peculiar habits and customs of the people. Any audience would be edified and delighted with him.

DONALD D. MAC LAURIN, D. D.,
Pastor Woodward Ave. Baptist Church, Detroit, Mich.

I have examined papers shown by Mr. Adams, Persian, who is seeking an education in this country for future usefulness, and find them good. Without personal knowledge of his antecedents, I take him to be what he claims, and trustworthy.

S. M. MERRILL,
Bishop M. E. Church, Chicago, Ill.

Mr. Isaac Adams gave his lecture on Persia, in the M. E. Church of our village, under the auspices of the Women's Foreign Missionary Society, and it was very entertaining and instructive and I heartily recommend him as a lecturer and Christian brother.

MRS. N. W. MATHER.
Pres't Big Rapids District, W. F. M. S., Howard City, Mich.

To Whom it May Concern: Brother Isaac Adams lectured to a large congregation here, composed of the Methodist and Baptist Churches. His lecture was very interesting and greatly appreciated. His coming has helped the missionary spirit among our people. Evidently the Lord is using him to do a great work in this country. Let all encourage him, and hear him.

E. L. SINCLEIR,
Pastor M. E. Church, Reed City, Mich.

Mr. Isaac Adams, a native Persian, spoke to a crowded house Sunday evening, February 26, 1893, to the great satisfaction of all. Our people are stirred on the missionary question as never before. Many remarked that they had always opposed foreign missionary work because they believed it the duty of the Church to care for the home work first, but hereafter they would pay their money where it would be most appreciated and accomplish the greatest amount of good. I very cordially commend Brother Adams to the Christian public everywhere as an earnest Christian gentleman, worthy of entire confidence and aid; he is preparing to return to his own people as a missionary.

FRANK H. NIX,
Pastor Morley M. E. Church, Morley, Mich.

This is to certify that Mr Isaac Adams gave a public address on the Religions and People of Persia, at a union meeting of the evangelical churches in the central part of our city on Sunday evening, July 2, 1893, to the edification of the people assembled. It is to be hoped that the way will soon be opened for the return of Mr. Adams to his native land, that he may preach the gospel to his own countrymen.   W. J JOHNSON,
Pastor First M. E. Church, Sioux City, Iowa.

MY DEAR MR. ADAMS: I enclose a letter of introduction for you to Rev. Dr. Johnson, of McCormick Theological Seminary. I think, that, upon reading it, he will give you opportunity for a full conversation with him, and I would advise you, before you call, to think over what you wish to say and arrange it somewhat in your mind, so that you will be able to set your matter before him fully and yet briefly. I shall always be glad to hear from you, and trust that God will direct your steps and keep you steadfast in his service and love.
ARTHUR MITCHELL, D. D.,
Sec'y Board of Foreign Missions, Presb. Church, New York.
(See page 30)

Mr. Isaac Adams, of Persia, spoke in our church twice on Sunday, May 8th, 1892, at the Christian Endeavor missionary meeting and at the regular service. The people were much interested He also gave a gospel address at the Y. M. C. A. meeting on the same day, which my young men said was an address of decided power. I can cordially commend this brother to any who may desire a missionary address on Persia.
JAMES LEWIS,
Pastor Central Presbyterian Church, Joliet, Ill.

Mr. Isaac Adams, a Nestorian from Oroomiah, Persia, comes to me with letters of commendation from Dr. Arthur Mitchell. He has spoken with success in my church. His purpose is one which commends itself to all and I hope he may meet with entire success.   HANFORD A. EDSON,
Memorial Church, Indianapolis, Ind.

TO THE METHODIST CLERGY: Isaac Adams is a success as a speaker. He addressed 1,000 people in my church on the evening of July 9, 1893, and we were all delighted You will make no mistake in giving him your pulpit.
FRANK CRANE, D. D.,
Pastor First M. E. Church of Omaha, Neb.

Mr. Isaac Adams is a native of Oroomiah, Persia, and is studying in this country to prepare himself for work in his native land. He has testimonials from Dr. Arthur Mitchell of our Foreign Board, from Dr. Wallace and other pastors of Chicago, and from Dr. Edson and others of Indianapolis. I can cheerfully commend him and his work to your favor.

REV. T L. HUGHES,

Shelbyville, Ind.

Mr. Isaac Adams, of Oroomiah, Persia, conducted the afternoon meeting for young men in the Young Men's Christian Association building on June 5, 1892. His address on the "Story of the Cross" was straightforward and simple and touched the hearts of all who heard him. Mr. Adams seems fully qualified in every way for the great and self-sacrificing work that he contemplates, mission work among his own people, the Nestorians. We all feel grateful to him for the inspiration of his remarks and heartily commend him to all Christian people as worthy of confidence.

E. A P. HAYNES,

Chairman Religious Work Committee, Indianapolis, Ind.

Brother Isaac Adams, who is preparing for medical missionary work and has several schools in Persia where the children are taught the principals of the Christian religion, has written of his past experiences, we have known him for several years and have found him a sincere and consecrated student in the worthy cause of Christian mission work and would commend his book and believe it will prove both interesting and instructive.

REV. J. C. VOORHIS,

Hackensack, N. J.

Brother Isaac Adams, an excellent Christian brother from Persia, who is deeply interested in the welfare of his people, I can give my hearty endorsement in his undertaking. I earnestly hope and pray that he will meet with great success, and that he may ultimately return and engage in his mission. I most cordially commend him and his work. Brother Adams is a young man of fine ability ; his purpose is to fit himself for greater usefulness for the cause of the Master and his people. Brother Adams is known to me for about five years, and I have every reason to believe that he is worthy of all confidence. I most heartily recommend his project to the Christian public or individuals who may feel interested to contribute something to the aid of his good work.

REV. G. E. BOER,

Prof. Christian Ref. Theol. Seminary, Grand Rapids, Mich.

Mr. Isaac Adams has been a frequent visitor at my home during the last three years, and I have been acquainted with him for four years. And I can heartily commend him and his work to all those who are interested in the advancement of God's Kingdom in Persia. I make that assertion both from the fact that I have taken considerable pains to examine into his character, and from personal experience in my association with him for three years. April 8, 1898.   REV. S. I. VANDERBEEK,
Pastor Christian Reformed Church, Grand Rapids, Mich.

I have known Isaac Adams for some time past; for five months he was in my employ. I have found him to be an intelligent, industrious, worthy, Christian young man, and worthy of any aid that will enable him to pursue his studies.
CAPT. W. H. MATHEWS,
Sup't Forty-fourth Street Boys' Lodging House, New York.

To Whom it May Concern: This certifies that I have known Isaac Adams for more than a year, and I consider him an earnest, reliable, Christian young man. He has been one year as a student at Hampton Normal Institute, Va., and his teachers there speak of him in the highest terms and are hopeful of his being able to return to his country, Persia, and be an instrument of good in teaching them of the higher ways of living. I most cheerfully recommend him to the confidence of any church desiring to help in foreign missionary work.
B. W. TICE,
Sup't West Side Boys' Lodging House, New York.

To Whom it May Concern: This is to certify that Isaac Adams, from Oroomiah, Persia, has been connected with this institution for eight months, and has been an earnest student and a straightforward Christian man. He is preparing himself for work among his own people.
REV. H. B. FRISSELL,
Chaplain Normal and Agricultural Institute, Hampton, Va.

To Any Concerned: Mr. Isaac Adams, a native of Persia, has stayed in our town a couple of months, and has spoken with much acceptance in all the leading churches, and in our hall, to large audiences. We take great pleasure in recommending him as a brother in Christ, worthy of the confidence and help of all Christian people, and wish him God-speed in his preparation for missionary work among his own people.
T. F. BEST,
Sec'y Young Men's Christian Association, Brantford, Canada.

ACKNOWLEDGMENT.

I feel very much indebted to several persons who have kindly aided me, a poor, forlorn stranger in this vast country, in publishing this little volume. To them all, in whatever way they may have been of assistance to me, I hereby tender my heartiest thanks, hoping that our common Lord and Savior, Jesus Christ, may let them reap returns as He has promised.

ISAAC ADAMS.

www.ingramcontent.com/pod-product-compliance
Lightning Source LLC
Chambersburg PA
CBHW031358020726
47499CB00005B/1447